cycle maintenance

cycle

hamlyn

Richard Hallett

maintenance

First published in Great Britain in 2002 by
Hamlyn, a division of Octopus Publishing Group Ltd
2–4 Heron Quays, London E14 4JP

Distributed in the United States and Canada by
Sterling Publishing Co., Inc.
387 Park Avenue South, New York, NY 10016-8810

ISBN 0 600 60676 7

A CIP catalogue record for this book is available from the
British Library

Printed and bound in China

10 9 8 7 6 5 4 3 2 1

Notes:
Conversions are given for all measurements, except
those relating to specific tools and components
which are only available in metric or imperial.

The photographs used are intended to illustrate the
key points in the step-by-step instructions. Where
instructions are particularly intricate, there are
several photographs for one step.

The publishers would like to thank **Madison Cycles**
for supplying the equipment featured in this
publication.
www.madisonbrandinformation.com

Contents

Introduction

Cycling is one of life's most enjoyable activities; whether it be commuting, competing or simply taking the family for a leisurely spin. But whatever your style of riding, a well-maintained machine will make it even more enjoyable. Bicycles are simple machines and, with a little know-how, they are straightforward to maintain.

This book will show you in clear, concise detail how to tackle every job from fitting a tyre to installing and adjusting the rear derailleur. The more complex components are individually identified, and there are sections on cleaning and servicing, and on the best selection of tools for the workshop and the roadside.

The maintenance tasks detailed are all within the abilities of the amateur mechanic, and the book is intended as a reference for beginners and the more experienced alike. If ever there was a time to learn to twirl a spanner, it is now!

Road racing bike stripped of all but vital components. Lightweight, high gears and aggressive riding position shout 'speed'.

Tourer. Equipped with mudguards, pannier rack and low gears for comfort and carrying capacity.

Folding bike. Designed to take up minimal space when not in use. Performance suffers as a result.

The bicycle labelled

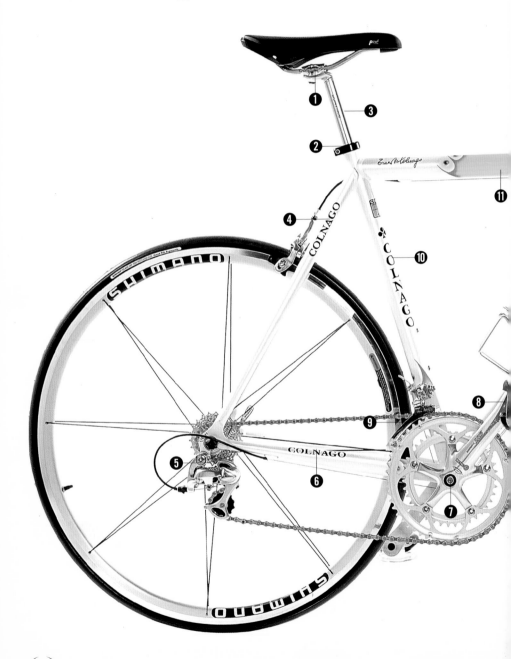

1. Saddle clamp
2. Seat-post clamp
3. Seat post
4. Seat stay
5. Rear mech
6. Chain stay
7. Chainset
8. Clipless pedals
9. Front mech
10. Seat tube
11. Top tube
12. Down tube
13. Head tube
14. Gear cable adjuster
15. Threadless stem
16. STI dual-function levers

Pre-ride inspection

The pre-ride inspection should be performed before the first ride of the day. It is your opportunity both to find and correct any problems sustained during the previous ride, and to ensure that the cycle runs reliably, safely and efficiently.

Time: 5 minutes
Grade of job: easy
Tools: track pump, cycle stand, chain lube

1 Start by lifting the front of the cycle and banging on the top of the front wheel to check that it is secure; vandals may easily tamper with quick-release levers, even during a short stop. Spin each wheel in turn, observing that it runs true and without play in the bearings and that the tyre is free of bulges, kinks and cuts.

2 Rock the saddle to ensure that it is secure.

Tip

If at the end of a ride in wet weather there is no time to clean the cycle properly, spray the chain with a water-dispersant lube before storage to prevent rusting and seizure.

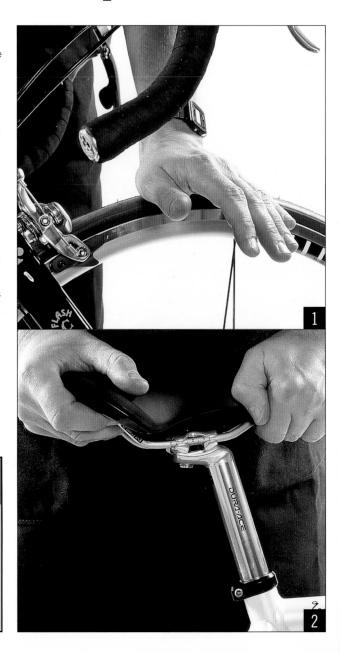

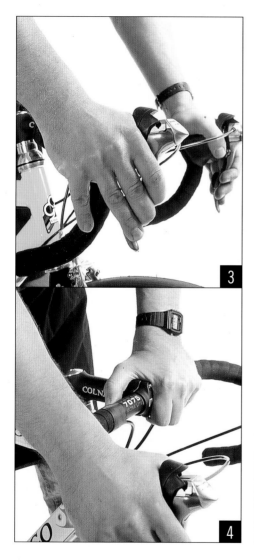

3 Pull on the brake levers, making sure that any quick-release mechanisms are closed and that the brake levers snap back cleanly into position. Check the wear left in the blocks, and then adjust free play if necessary.

4 Pull on the front brake and rock the machine back and forth to look for play in the head-bearing.

5 With the cycle in a stand, turn the pedals and run through the entire range of gears. Look for poor shifting, seized links and any hint that the chain is jumping. Where necessary, lubricate the chain and adjust the gear indexing.

6 Finally, inflate both tyres to your preferred pressure.

Toolkits

Use of the correct tools will make any maintenance task easier, less hazardous and more enjoyable. Working with ill-fitting tools risks damage to cycle parts and to hands and fingers.

The workshop toolkit

The contents of a workshop toolkit should cover the tasks its owner feels competent to tackle. Advanced tools such as those for cutting threads, facing bearing-seats and pressing cartridge bearings fall outside the scope of this book, but the maintenance procedures explained may all be carried out using the readily available hand tools shown. A vice, workbench and selection of household tools – such as a hacksaw, half-round file, hammer and screwdrivers – will help with many jobs.

The roadside toolkit

A well-maintained cycle used on the road should need little attention beyond puncture repair and fine-tuning of gears. The basic roadside toolkit should include spare inner tubes, tyre levers and a puncture repair kit. It is also advisable to carry a suitable set of Allen keys. On longer rides and tours, add a spare folding tyre and a chain-splitting tool, especially when riding in remote areas.

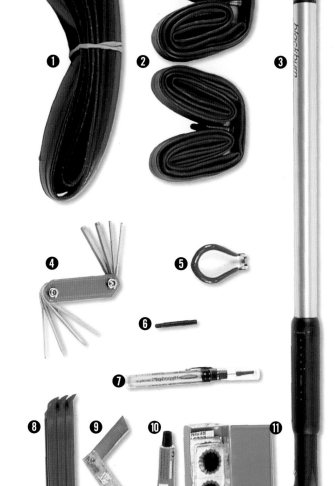

1. Folding tyre
2. Inner tubes
3. Frame-fitting pump
4. Allen key set
5. Spoke key
6. Valve extender
7. Oil
8. Tyre levers
9. Instant patch
10. Rubber solution
11. Puncture repair kit

Wheel removal and replacement

A quick-release (QR) wheel lever not only speeds wheel removal and replacement but also, when correctly operated, provides a safer, more reliable means of securing either wheel than a hex or wing-nut. Cycles may be provided with 'nutted' axles for reasons of cost, or for use on a velodrome where potentially dangerous protrusions are not allowed. Nuts should be checked frequently for security and tightened using the correct size socket or ring spanner.

QR front wheel removal and replacement

Time: 30 seconds
Grade of job: simple
Tools: none

1 Slacken any brake QR mechanism. Shimano brakes use a lever on the caliper, while Campagnolo units use a button on the Ergo Power brake lever.

2 Hook the right thumb around the QR lever and open it outwards. The wheel should fall free of the fork dropouts. If not, the dropouts may have small lips designed to hold an inadequately secured wheel. In this case, unscrew the QR nut on the left-hand side of the hub until there is enough clearance around each lip. You can then remove the wheel.

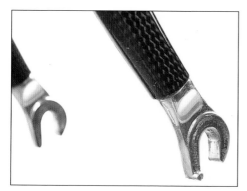

Dropouts with integral lips offer failsafe security.

3 To refit the wheel, hold the handlebars in one hand and the top of the wheel in the other, drop the fork over the wheel, slide the tyre between the brake blocks and align the dropouts with the hub lock-nuts. Lower the dropouts into place and let the fork rest centrally on the wheel spindle

4 If fitting a new wheel or a wheel to a fork with 'safety lips', readjust the QR nut. Position the QR lever so that it will close in front of the fork blade, and then hold it open just above the horizontal. Now screw in the nut until it touches the opposite dropout, and close the lever. If this action requires excessive force, open the lever and slacken the nut one-quarter of a turn. Close the lever. Repeat this adjustment until the lever can be closed fully by the application of comfortable pressure.

5 Finally, close the brake QR mechanism.

Removal and replacement of QR rear wheel

Time: 1 minute
Grade of job: easy
Tools: none

1 Engage top gear and turn the pedals to shift the chain to the smallest sprocket.

2 Undo the QR brake and wheel levers, lift the rear of the cycle and allow the wheel to drop down. Should the cassette rest on the chain, push the rear mech's jockey-wheel cage down to disengage it.

3 To replace the wheel, ensure that the rear mech is shifted to top gear by operating the dual-control or down-tube shift lever. Hold the cycle high enough to position the wheel within the rear stays. Thread the cassette inside the chain loop. Lower the cycle, guiding the top of the wheel between the brake blocks. Install the chain on the smallest sprocket; the dropouts will now be aligned with the hub lock-nuts and the wheel will drop into place. If not, then the chain stays may be too short; compress the tyre by pushing the wheel forwards as it drops down.

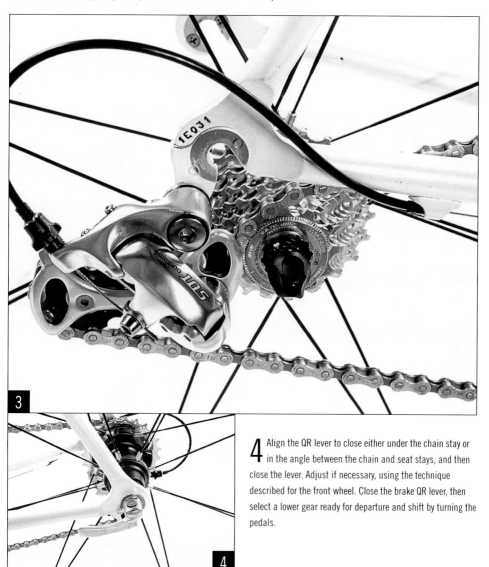

3

4 Align the QR lever to close either under the chain stay or in the angle between the chain and seat stays, and then close the lever. Adjust if necessary, using the technique described for the front wheel. Close the brake QR lever, then select a lower gear ready for departure and shift by turning the pedals.

4

Tyre removal and replacement

Removing and refitting a clincher bicycle tyre is a straightforward process provided the correct technique is followed. Tyre levers should be used during removal, although they should not be used for fitment, since the risk of pinching and puncturing the inner tube is high.

Removal of tyre and tube

Time: 2 minutes
Grade of job: easy
Tools: tyre levers

1 Proceed around the deflated tyre, pushing its bead into the well of the rim on both sides. Position the wheel with the valve at the top and insert the first tyre lever immediately to its right. The curved lip of the lever must slide under the bead.

2 Insert the second lever approximately 150mm (6in) further round to the right, and then pull the first lever downwards, easing the bead over the rim. If this is excessively difficult, check that the tyre at the opposite point of the wheel (at the bottom) is fully pushed into the well. Now repeat with the second lever.

3 A section of the bead will now be visible outside the rim, and it will be tight enough to stay there. Repeat the lever motion to the right several times until the bead becomes loose, then slide a finger or lever between the inside of the bead and the rim and run it all the way around to displace the tyre completely. The inner tube can now be pulled free; finish at the valve. At this point, a new tube can be fitted.

4 Finally, use fingers to pull the other bead over the rim to the same side.

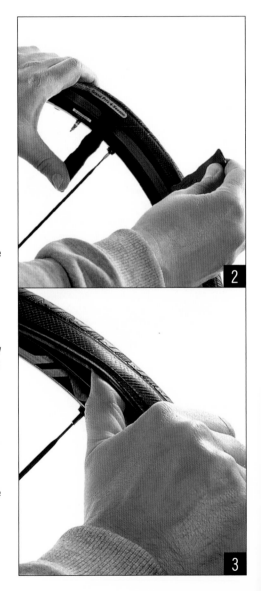

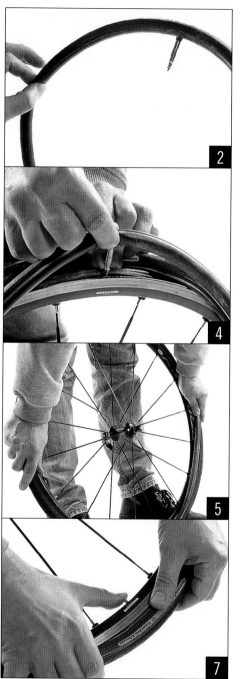

Fitting tyre and tube

Time: 5 minutes
Grade of job: moderate
Tools: talcum powder or French chalk

1 Thoroughly dust the inside of the tyre with chalk. Place the bead that is farthest away from you over the lip of the rim, then work it around on both sides until fully in place. The tyre may become tight towards the end, so seat the bead firmly in the rim well at the starting point.

2 Lightly inflate the inner tube to hold its shape without any increase in diameter, and then dust it thoroughly with chalk.

3 In one hand hold the wheel with the valve hole at the top, the open side of the tyre facing away, and the non-fitted bead pulled back to reveal the valve hole. Rest the tyre on your feet to create a trough that will protect the tube from grit. Hold the tube with the valve at the top and lower the bottom run into the tyre.

4 Insert the valve into its hole and cover the tube with the tyre all round the wheel. Do not fit the tyre at this point.

5 Now turn the wheel around and, starting opposite the valve, pull the bead over the rim and ease it into place inside the well. Work the tyre into place on both sides; the bead will stretch tight just before you reach the valve.

6 Now deflate the tube and push the bead into the centre of the rim well at your start point; this will slacken the bead enough for it to be pushed over the rim using thumbs.

7 As the last 25mm (1in) of bead is about to pop home, push the valve back into the rim. Push the bead home, then press the valve back down from the outside of the tyre and inflate.

8 Spin the wheel and check that the tyre runs straight; if there is any wobble in the tread and carcass, deflate the tyre and reseat it before inflating again.

Tube and tyre repairs

Punctured inner tubes may be repaired using either traditional or instant, pre-glued patches. The former produce a more permanent repair, and a tube may be patched several times this way before being regarded as unfit for use. Tubes should not be repaired if the cut or hole is so close to the valve that the patch overlaps the edge of the valve, nor should two patches overlap. In an emergency, a severe cut in a tyre may be 'booted' (repaired with a square of canvas or a special kit), although this should only ever be used as a temporary measure. A booted repair may be used where the tyre has a hole or cut that allows the inner tube to bulge through and burst. Never inflate a booted tyre to more than half its normal recommended pressure; perhaps less if the cut is exceptionally long.

Tube repair using a conventional patch

Time: 5 minutes
Grade of job: easy
Tools: puncture repair outfit

Try to narrow down the site of a puncture before the tube is removed. Examine the tread for embedded flints or for air escaping through a cut. If a problem is found, note its position relative to the valve.

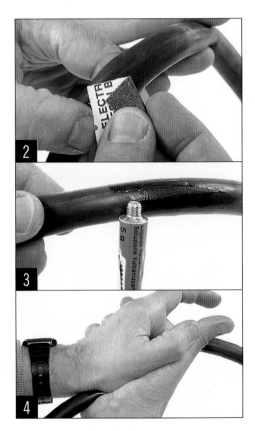

1 If the puncture is not obvious, inflate the tube and run it slowly past your lips until the escaping air is felt. As a last resort, dip the tube in water and look for escaping bubbles. Dry the tube thoroughly before attempting a repair. Circle the cut with yellow wax crayon (not essential).

2 Using glass paper, scrub the surface of the tube for at least 25mm (1in) around the cut until all chalk is removed.

3 Apply a thin coat of rubber solution and allow to dry for a few minutes. Inflate the tyre gently; a bubble of solution will reveal the location of the cut, enabling precise patch application.

4 Remove the foil from the patch and place it centrally over the cut. Place the tube between your palms and apply firm, even pressure to the patch and tube for one minute.

5 Pinch the patch to split the backing film, and peel the film away from the centre of the patch outwards.

Tips

- Slow punctures can be very hard to solve. Air loss can be caused by a leaking valve, or a spot on the tube rubbed thin by friction with the tyre. A faulty valve usually means the tube is beyond repair.

- For easy storage, roll the tube up with the valve open to expel air, then close the valve.

Tube repair using an instant patch

Time: 1 minute
Grade of job: easy
Tools: instant patch

Follow steps 1 and 2 (left). Peel the patch from its backing film, position over the cut and press firmly into place.

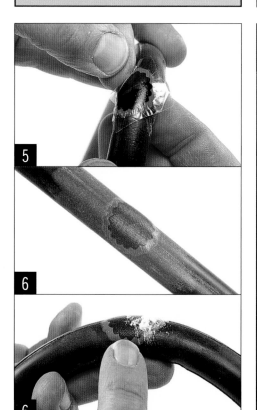

5

6

6

6 Dust the area around the repair with chalk before refitting or storage.

Booting a tyre

Time: 5 minutes
Grade of job: moderate
Tools: booting kit or puncture repair kit with canvas patch

Select a piece of canvas or a booting patch big enough to cover the cut with at least 12mm (½in) of material to spare at each end.

1 If using a kit, follow the gluing instructions. If using a piece of canvas, coat the patch liberally with solution.

2 Clean the inside of the tyre and coat the area around the cut with plenty of solution.

3 Allow the solution to dry on both patch and tyre, and then position the patch carefully before pressing into place.

4 Put the booted tyre between your palms and apply firm, even pressure for one minute.

5 Dust the repaired area with chalk before refitting the tyre.

Cable installation

Control cables are the nervous system of the bicycle; let them deteriorate and both braking and gear shifting will feel sluggish, remote and unresponsive. Modern cables are usually fitted with low-friction Teflon liners around a stainless-steel inner wire. These cables are long lasting and need little regular maintenance beyond inspection for fraying. Surviving examples of older, non-lined cables should always be replaced with newer cables.

A typical brake outer casing has a conventional, close-spiral winding under the plastic sheath, is designed to run easily around curves and may be recognized by the single strand visible at a cut end. By contrast, a gear casing, which is designed to resist compression, comprises many wires running parallel along its length. These may be seen at the cut end.

End caps should always be fitted to the tips of inner wires to prevent hazardous and unsightly fraying. To avoid the risk of a breakage, never re-clamp an inner wire at a previous clamping point, and if re-using an inner wire always clamp it nearer the nipple to avoid pulling on the section deformed by clamping. Only use a dedicated cable cutter for the inner wire; side-cutting pliers will squash and splay the ends and will not cut cleanly.

The cut end of an outer brake casing will often show a distorted hook that obscures the opening; this must be clipped off before the casing is used. The end may be ground flat using a grinding wheel if available. Outer gear casing will compress to an oval after cutting; it should be pressed back into a circle. The Teflon liner can be opened up with a pick if deformed.

Installing a brake cable

Time: 15 minutes
Grade of job: moderate
Tools: cable cutter, crimping pliers, Allen keys, grease

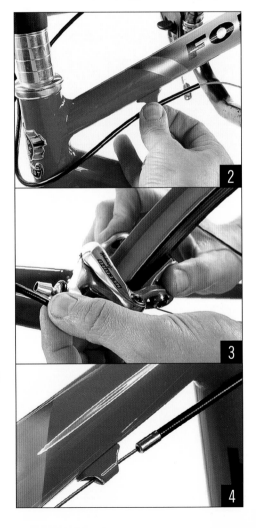

1 When fitting brake cables it is also advisable to fit new brake blocks (see page 31) and to check that any threaded play-adjuster is backed off to its minimum setting to ensure proper initial play adjustment.

2 Insert one end of the cable's outer casing into the brake-lever housing, and then run the casing to its first stop. On the front brake, this will be at the caliper itself. Allow enough length for a smooth, clean curve at all points. The front section of casing for the rear brake and for dual-function gear cables must have enough length to allow the handlebars to turn fully to both sides without snagging.

3 If the rear brake needs a further length of casing from a second frame stop to the caliper, squeeze the brake blocks against the rim and cut enough casing to run easily to the caliper in this position.

4 Now cut the casing and trim the end flat. Fit a ferrule to the tip of the casing at the brake cable stop (note: some cable stops may not provide enough room for a ferrule).

5 Remove the outer casing from the brake lever housing, and then install the inner wire. Lightly grease the inner wire and thread it through the outer casing. Thread the inner wire through the caliper adjuster and cable clamp. Squeeze the blocks against the rim, release them by about 5mm (¼in), and then lightly tighten the cable clamp screw.

6 Pull on the brake lever to seat the casings. If the blocks are now too far from the rim, release the inner wire clamp and repeat the previous step. Final adjustment should let the blocks touch the rim a little less than halfway through the brake lever travel. Cut the inner wire about 50mm (2in) below the clamp, install the end cap and secure it by crimping in several places.

Installing a gear cable

Time: 15 minutes
Grade of job: moderate
Tools: cable cutters, crimping pliers, Allen keys, grease

1 This process is much the same as for brake cables. However, all outer casing ends must be fitted with ferrules to ensure accurate shifting.

2

2 Since the inner wire is thinner than that used for brakes, use the correct end caps for a snug fit.

3 Grease the inner wire where it passes through a guide under the bottom-bracket shell, and grease the nipple to ensure that is does not corrode inside its housing.

Cleaning and lubricating the cycle

Regular cleaning will not only keep your cycle looking good but will also ensure that it continues to run smoothly and efficiently. Cleaning your cycle also gives you an opportunity to look out for excessive or unusual wear, and for indicators of potential failure such as cracks and areas worn smooth by rubbing. If used exclusively in fine conditions, a cycle may only need cleaning every few months; ridden daily in poor weather, it will need a wash at least once a week.

Clean and lube

Time: 30 minutes
Grade of job: easy
Tools: cycle stand, water-soluble degreaser, bike cleaner, car shampoo, buckets, sponge, various brushes

1 Start by removing the rear wheel and placing the cycle in a stand. Fit a chain retainer or place a screwdriver between the rear dropouts to hold the chain at a comfortable angle.

2 Work degreaser into the chain using a stiff brush. Degreaser should also be applied to any area contaminated by chain lube including the cage plates of the front derailleur and the rear-wheel sprockets.

3 Spray the whole machine with bike wash and use a sponge to wash it down with liberal quantities of hot water and shampoo. Scrub handlebar tape and the saddle with a brush if necessary. Use bottle brushes to reach into small gaps.

4 Remove the front wheel and wash down the inside of the fork blades.

5 Run the sponge firmly around each tyre and rim in turn to remove all grit and dirt from the tyre sidewalls. Wash spokes individually, starting and finishing at the valve.

6 Soak a large piece of sponge with soapy water, hold it around a section of the chain and turn the pedal to pull the chain through the sponge, which should be squeezed to wash water over the chain. Repeat this process until all the degreaser has been washed out of the chain.

7 Fill a bucket with clean water and throw a wave of water over the cycle to rinse off the soap. Repeat from the opposite end of the cycle.

8 Rinse the wheels, and then spray the spindle ends and QR lever parts with a water-dispersing lubricant or similar before refitting. Run the chain through a clean, dry rag before spraying it with the same lube to drive out water; run it through the rag again to absorb excess spray.

9 Allow the chain to dry and then apply a thick, specialist chain lube. Spray lubricant on all moving parts, pivots and bearings in the gear mechs and brake calipers to protect them from corrosion, and then wipe down the paintwork with a clean, dry cloth or chamois.

Tip

Do not spray lube near the rims or brake blocks.

Cup-and-cone bearings

Ball or roller bearings are used in many parts of the bicycle. The modern trend is to use annular or cartridge bearings, which cannot be serviced. When wear becomes apparent, either through rough running or noticeable play, they should be replaced. Where bearings must be replaced as individual cartridges, the job requires specialist bearing-driving tools and is best performed by a skilled mechanic.

Traditionally, bicycles were fitted with cup-and-cone bearings, which have separate balls and are adjusted by moving one bearing face, either cup or cone, along a thread before securing it in position with a lock-ring or nut. Found in the hubs, pedals, bottom bracket and headset, cup-and-cone bearings are easily serviced, and the balls and bearing surfaces may be replaced when worn. Regular servicing, depending on the severity of usage, will ensure a long life. The example below is for a hub bearing, but the principle applies to all such bearings. For a clearer view of the headset, see page 98.

Servicing cup-and-cone hub bearings

Time: 45 minutes
Grade of job: difficult
Tools: cone and lock-nut spanners, small screwdriver, spindle clamp, rag, grease

1 Slacken and remove the lock-nut on one end of the spindle, noting the orientation of any knurled marks. Remove the washer and then the cone to reveal the balls on one side.

2 Hold the wheel over a clean rag and drop the spindle through. Some balls may follow it. Those that remain should be poked down the barrel of the hub. Turn the wheel over and remove any remaining balls.

3 Clean the balls and bearing surfaces with a clean rag. Pack the inside of the cups with grease and then install the balls. Count the balls first and fit half to each side.

4 Slide the spindle, complete with undisturbed cone and nuts, through the barrel of the hub until it seats against the balls. Rotate the spindle a few times to ensure that the balls are correctly positioned, and then invert the wheel while holding the spindle.

5 Screw the remaining cone into place against its own balls, and then refit the washer and lock-nut with any gripping indents on the outside.

6 Adjust the cone to remove play without making the bearing run roughly, and then tighten the lock-nut with moderate force against the cone.

7 If this makes the bearing run roughly, place a spanner on each of the cones and turn them anti-clockwise until it runs smoothly. Now fully tighten the lock-nut.

Tip

To make working on the hub easier, hold the end of the spindle in a spindle clamp secured in a vice.

Rims and spokes

Wheel rims are one of the most highly stressed parts of the bike. They have to run straight and true while absorbing constant impacts and acting as one half of the braking system.

The action of the brake blocks has the effect of wearing through the sidewalls of the rim. When these become too thin to resist the pressure, the rim can burst halfway down and jam against the brake blocks. Therefore, the braking surface of the rim should be checked frequently. If the area touched by the blocks is found to have worn inwards by more than 1mm (¹⁄₂₅in), the rim must be replaced.

Spokes are apt to break at the least convenient moment, throwing the rim out of true and weakening the wheel further. If out on the road without a spare spoke, the brake QR mechanism may be opened to gain clearance. In the event of a severe kink in the rim, the two spokes immediately to each side of the broken spoke may be slackened by half a turn until it can be replaced. Wheelbuilding is an art and for best results should be learnt through first-hand tuition or a book dedicated to the subject.

Spoke replacement and wheel truing

Time: 15 minutes
Grade of job: moderate/difficult
Tools: spoke key, spoke gauge, tyre levers, cassette removal tools

If a spoke breaks at the hub, it may be unscrewed from the nipple without disturbing the rim tape. If, however, it breaks leaving a portion of thread inside the nipple, the tape will have to be removed.

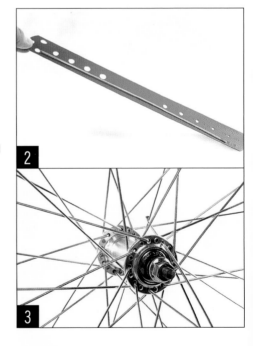

1 Start by removing the tyre and tube, and then the spoke. With the rear wheel this may be impossible without first removing the sprockets.

2 Measure the spoke either with a ruler (from the inside of the bend to the tip of the thread) or with a spoke gauge. Alternatively, take the spoke to a shop. Obtain the same type of spoke (for example, double butted or plain gauge). Always use the correct length spoke when making a permanent repair.

3 Thread the spoke through the hub flange. If unsure from which side, note the orientation of the spokes on either side. They exit on alternate sides, and the new one must do the same.

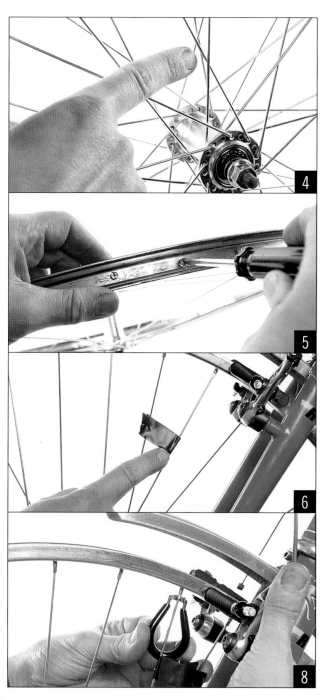

4 Lace the spoke through those it crosses. Again, note the positioning of the adjacent spokes on the same side running in the same direction, and copy them.

5 Thread the spoke into the nipple and tighten the nipple initially with a screwdriver from the outside of the rim. Viewed from this point, the spoke tightens clockwise.

6 Wrap a piece of tape around the spoke for identification and continue to tighten it to almost the same tension as those adjacent.

7 Install the wheel in the cycle and turn it. The wheel will almost certainly have a small wobble at the new spoke nipple.

8 Compare the rim against a brake block. If the rim moves towards the new spoke side, slacken the spoke slightly; if it moves away from the new spoke, it should be tightened. Proceed by one-quarter of a turn when adjusting spoke tension.

Identify your brakes

Road-going bicycles almost invariably employ light, easily maintained brakes that act on the rims. Internal hub brakes are used on some utility machines for their durability and minimal maintenance needs. In both cases, operation is still by wire cables. Of the many rim-acting brakes ever designed, four are still in common use, and each has its merits. The **sidepull caliper brake** is simple to install but has been largely superseded by the more powerful **dual-pivot sidepull caliper**.

The **cantilever brake** offers greatly improved clearance for tyres and mudguards, and is popular on touring and tandem bicycles. It requires a separate straddle wire, and can only be fitted to frames with special mounting bosses.

V-brakes (also known as direct-pull brakes) are very powerful and easy to adjust. They are most commonly seen on hybrid and mountain bikes, and they need the same mounting bosses as cantilever brakes but not the straddle wire.

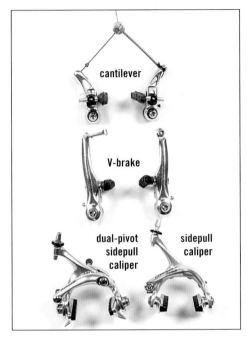

Brake blocks

Rim brakes work by pushing rubber blocks against the rim to generate friction. The blocks may be moulded in a harder or softer compound depending on expected service life and effectiveness, but while harder compounds last longer they tend to wear through rims more quickly. Blocks may be moulded complete with mounting fitments or made to sit in separate shoes. If the blocks are allowed to wear down too far, the backing plate, shoe or internal moulded support will touch the rim, markedly reducing braking effectiveness and scoring the rim.

Brake blocks wear most rapidly in wet, gritty conditions. They should be inspected frequently, and any grit stuck in the block removed. Most blocks are marked with a minimum wear line; if not, then replace the block when any grooves on the braking surface are no longer visible. Rim brakes should be centred (i.e. adjusted so that both blocks touch the rim simultaneously) to maximize feel and braking efficiency.

Installing new brake blocks

Time: 15 minutes
Grade of job: moderate
Tools: Allen keys or ring spanner as appropriate

1 Take the cycle to a shop if unsure of which type of brake block to buy. Slacken any cable adjusters to allow space for the new blocks, and then open the QR mechanism if working on caliper brakes (see page 32). Remove one old block at a time, complete with shoe if provided. This will allow you to check alignment when refitting.

2 If the blocks sit in shoes, check for any retaining grub screw; if found, remove this before sliding the old block out.

3 Install a new block in the shoe, observing directional indicators, and then refit the grub screw.

4 Offer the block up to the caliper or lever arm. Ensure that the open end of the shoe faces backwards. Pinch the caliper arms to hold the block against the rim if there is no toe-in alignment.

5 Align the top of the block parallel with the top of the rim, making sure that it sits about 3mm (⅛in) below the top of the rim. This will prevent a lip forming on the top of the block, which could wear through the tyre sidewall.

6 Tighten the securing nut or bolt and then recheck alignment.

7 Some Campagnolo blocks have an orbital mounting that permits adjustment of toe-in. Make sure that the mounting moves freely before tightening. Hold the block in position with a small degree of toe-in and then tighten the securing nut. Check alignment and readjust as necessary before tightening the nut fully.

8 Install the second block.

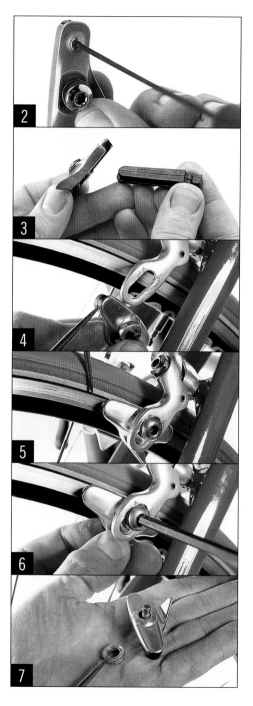

Sidepull and dual-pivot calipers

Both sidepull and dual-pivot calipers are fitted in the same way; only the centring adjustment differs. Older examples may be secured to the frame using an external hexagonal nut, however, current practice is to use a long 'top hat' nut with an Allen key head inside the frame. The two are not interchangeable between their respective frames.

Installation of dual-pivot caliper brakes

Time: 20 minutes
Grade of job: moderate
Tools: cycle stand, Allen keys or ring spanners as appropriate

1 Push the centre bolt through the frame- or fork-mounting hole and secure it lightly with the correct nut.

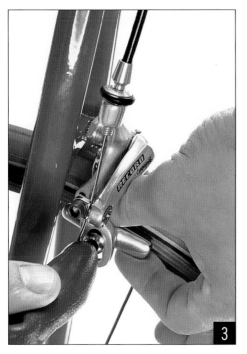

2 The caliper may be supplied with spacers or toothed anti-
slip washers; use as many of these as necessary to
ensure that the caliper arms clear any nearby frame parts.
Some carbon-fibre forks have very deep crowns that may
require the fitment of a long 'top hat' nut. Never install a
brake caliper using a nut that does not engage the centre bolt
thread for at least three turns.

3 Provisionally adjust the brake blocks, and then pinch
them against the rim while threading the cable's inner
wire through the adjuster and clamp bolt.

4 Lightly tighten the clamp bolt, and adjust both blocks as
detailed on page 30.

5 Adjust the brake cable play as detailed on page 22, and
then tighten the clamp bolt.

6 Holding the caliper roughly centred, fully tighten the
centre-bolt nut.

Centring dual-pivot brakes

Time: 1 minute
Grade of job: easy
Tools: Allen key or small screwdriver as appropriate

1 Shimano dual-pivot calipers are adjusted using the small screw on top of the long, front lever arm.

2 Campagnolo dual-pivot calipers are adjusted using the screw on the outside of the 'Y' arm. In either case, the aim is to have both blocks touch the rim at the same time.

3 Turn the screw, watching which way the brake blocks move. Both will move at once. Adjust the caliper so that they appear positioned equidistant from the rim, and then lightly apply the brake.

4 Watch to see whether one of the blocks touches first. If so, adjust it using the screw and recheck.

5 The job is complete when both blocks touch at once. The process should be carried out whenever the brake's free play is adjusted or new blocks are fitted.

Centring sidepull calipers

Time: 1 minute
Grade of job: easy
Tools: cone spanner, steel drift and hammer

1 Sidepull calipers use one spring to push both brake arms back from the rim at once. The vital spring is housed in the centre brake boss. Equal positioning of the arms of the spring centres the caliper arms.

2 Almost all sidepull calipers have machined faces on the centre boss, allowing it to be turned using a spanner. Find a spanner of suitable jaw size. A cone spanner is usually required to fit in the narrow gap.

3 Place the spanner over the flats on the centre boss and simply turn the whole caliper to realign the blocks equidistant from the sides of the rim.

4 Ensure that the brake centre bolt nut is tight.

5 Calipers without flats can be centred by striking the spring on one side of the centre boss. Apply a drift to the top surface of the spring on the same side as the brake block further from the rim, and tap it smartly to nudge the block closer. Repeat as often as necessary.

3

4

Cantilever brakes

The action of cantilever brakes is affected by many variables, including the angle from the cable stop to the straddle wire and the angle between the two sides of the straddle wire itself. As the brake blocks wear, they tend to run away from the rim's braking surface and need to be adjusted frequently for rim alignment to prevent them pushing under the rim. Low-profile cantilevers are the most common today; in this type of unit the blocks are mounted on a post, and the attachment to the arms allows adjustment over a wide range. For this reason, exceptional care is needed during block adjustment.

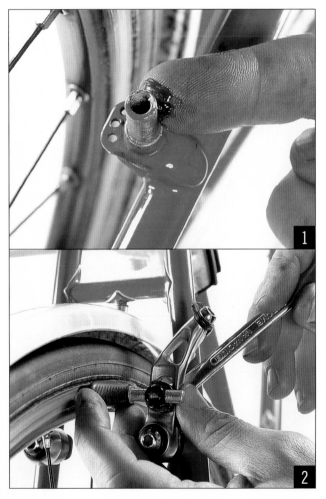

Cantilever installation and adjustment

Time: 30 minutes
Grade of job: moderate
Tools: Allen keys, ring spanners, cable cutter

1 Grease the boss and install both arms. Each frame boss has a choice of three holes for the spring tip; choose the hole that provides spring resistance when the block is still about 25mm (1in) from the rim.

2 Tighten the long centre pivot bolts. Provisionally install the brake blocks equally, clamping each post about 12mm (½in) from the outer face of the block.

3 Install the nipple end of the straddle wire, and insert the inner through the straddle-wire button and housing. Now pass it through the clamp on the right-hand arm, and squeeze the arms together while pulling the inner wire through the housing.

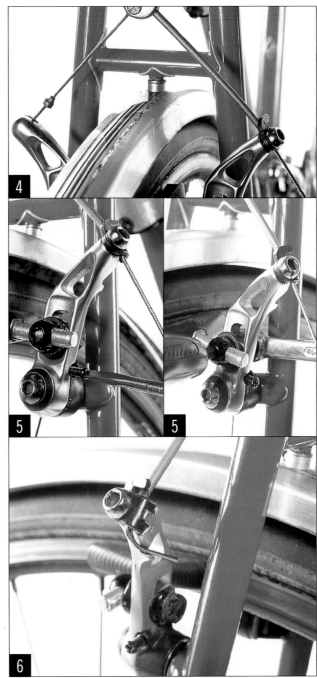

4 When the two sides of the straddle
wire are at roughly 90 degrees,
clamp the inner wire. Push the housing
hard against the clamp, and then ease
the inner wire over the angled peg on
the button until it sits in the groove.

5 Use the small screws on the
outside of the arms to centre the
blocks. If centring cannot be perfected
within the range of adjustment of the
springs, get it as close as possible. Now
slacken the brake shoes and reposition
them 2–3mm (⅛in) from the rim, with
the same gap on both sides. Tighten the
nut behind the arm fully once the blocks
are correctly aligned in all directions.

6 Squeeze the brake lever hard to
ensure every part is secure. Cut the
inner wire about 50mm (2in) from the
clamp, and tuck it away inside the arm.

V-brakes

The lack of a straddle wire makes V-brakes simple to install. The outer casing from the brake lever leads into a curved 'noodle' pipe, which sits in a link on the left-hand arm. To operate the QR function, pinch the blocks together and unship the noodle pipe from the link. When performing the reverse function, ensure that the noodle pipe end is properly installed before using the brake.

V-brake installation and adjustment

Time: 30 minutes
Grade of job: easy
Tools: Allen keys, cable cutters

1 Grease the frame bosses and install both arms, temporarily aligning the brake blocks along the arms for ease of installation. Tighten the long centre-bolts. V-brake blocks use spherical housings for maximum adjustability, and they have interchangeable thick and thin washers.

2 Position one arm vertically and align the block with the rim. If it is more than 3mm (⅛in) from the rim, separate the block mounting kit, noting the order of fitment, and swap the positions of the two washers described. They both have a concave surface, which mates with a convex washer. If the arm has to be pulled back from the rim, swap washers in the reverse manner.

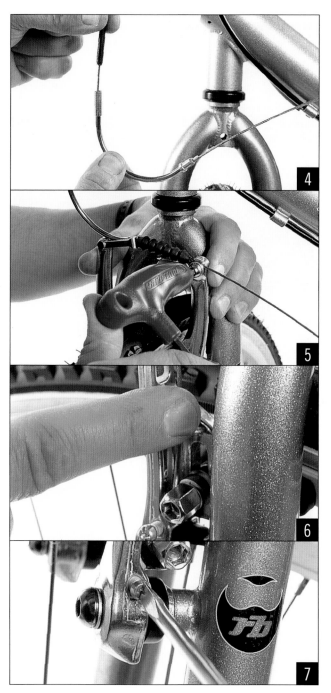

3 Align and tighten the brake blocks. Repeat for the other arm, making sure that the thick and thin washers are positioned symmetrically.

4 Cut the cable outer casing to length. Thread the inner wire through the noodle pipe, position the noodle pipe in its link and run the inner wire through the clamp on the right-hand arm.

5 Hold the brake arms together, ensuring that they remain parallel or angled slightly apart at the top. Clamp the inner wire, leaving a gap of 3mm (⅛in) between each block and the rim.

6 Cut the inner wire long enough to run behind the arm and inside the brake-block housing.

7 Check brake-block alignment, and adjust brake free play at the handlebar lever. Centre the brake using small adjuster screws.

Hub brakes and gears

Internal hub brakes and gears require minimal maintenance since their sealed design excludes dirt and water, thereby guaranteeing a low rate of wear. As with any cable-operated system, control cables must be replaced when damaged, and some disassembly is often required when a wheel is removed.

Installation of hub brake cable

Time: 10 minutes
Grade of job: easy
Tools: cable cutter, ring spanner, pliers

1 Cut the outer casing to length, and install the lightly greased inner wire. Run this through the cable adjuster and brake actuating-arm, giving it a clean, snag-free run.

2 Pull the arm towards the adjuster until the brake engages, release by about 5mm (¼in), and clamp the inner wire.

3 Cut to leave a small length spare, and crimp an end cap in place. When removing the wheel, try to avoid undoing the inner-wire clamp if possible; some hub brake systems allow the brake to separate from the hub.

Installation of hub gear cable

Time: 10 minutes
Grade of job: easy
Tools: cable cutter, ring spanner, pliers

1 Many hub gears rely on a toggle chain to transmit the pull on the inner wire to the inside of the hub. To find the correct length for the cable, shift the handlebar trigger to the highest gear and pull the inner wire taut.

2 Install the toggle chain in the hub and screw it home; aligning it with the direction of the inner wire by turning it back up to half a turn if necessary.

3 Turn the pedals once forwards to ensure the hub is in top gear, and then join the inner wire and toggle chain using the junction supplied.

4 Take up any slack in the chain and inner wire, but do not pre-tension the chain. Test by shifting at the trigger and turning the pedals to ascertain that the hub is engaging each gear.

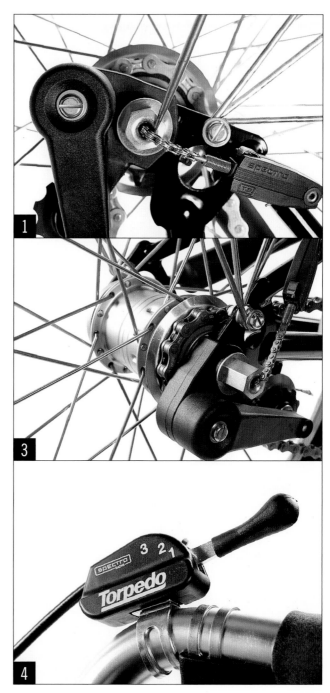

Brake levers

The position of brake levers on the handlebars affects both comfort and braking efficiency. With both flat and drop handlebars the aim should be to place the levers at an angle comfortable for the wrists and hands, and to have both levers at precisely the same height. Modern drop-handlebar brake levers are designed to keep the brake cable against the bars for aerodynamic and practical reasons. The cables on older drop-bar levers run vertically through the lever body into the open air before returning to the brakes; such cables are simple to install but are prone to bending and fraying.

Installation of aero brake levers and concealed cables

Time: 40 minutes
Grade of job: moderate
Tools: Allen keys, cable cutters, insulating tape

1 Pull back the rubber hood on the lever housing and find the clamping Allen nut. Unscrew the nut to free the clamping band, and slide the band onto the bar.

2 With an Allen key in the nut head, offer the nut up to the screw in the clamp band and tighten it enough to keep the lever assembly in place.

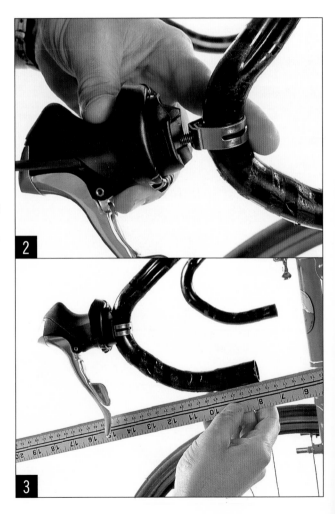

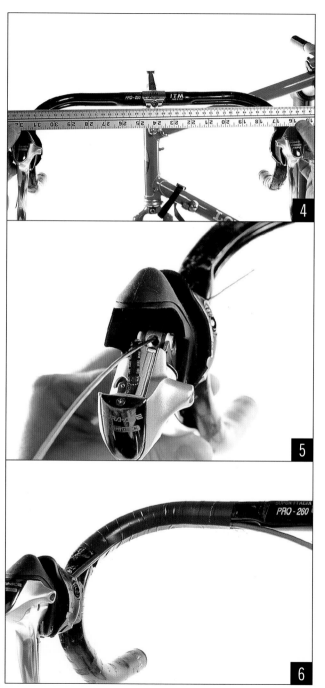

3 Use a rule to align the first brake lever. For conventionally curved bars with brake-only levers, it is suggested that the tip be aligned with the underside of the bar. For Shimano dual-function levers with 'anatomic' bars, try aligning the underside of the bar with the curve on the end of the lever. Check that your hand can reach the lever while holding the drop section and sitting in the saddle. If not, the lever can often be brought closer to the bar by moving it up or down a little. Tighten the clamp nut firmly, but not to the maximum; in a crash, a lever that moves slightly is less likely to bend.

4 Repeat the installation process for the second lever, but align it with the first, rather than with the handlebar. To do this, run the rule across an equivalent point on the two lever bodies, and align it with the top run of the handlebars. Move the second lever up or down until both are in line. Firmly tighten the second lever's clamp nut.

5 Install the complete inner wire and outer casing for the first lever (see page 22). If fitting Campagnolo Ergo Power levers, install the shift cables as detailed on page 44 before continuing. Otherwise, position the brake cable in the handlebar groove if available, or run it along the front of the bar if not.

6 Then, starting at the lever end, tape the cable tightly to the bar along its length to a point 20mm (¾in) from the start of the bar's centre bulge.

7 Repeat on the other side.

Dual-function levers

Dual-function shift and brake levers have revolutionized the use of derailleur gears; substituting crisp, precise and accurate fingertip gear changing in place of the knack required to use friction down-tube levers. Dual-function levers are part of an indexed gear system that requires precise adjustment, and which can be spoilt from the beginning by poor cable installation. See page 22 for details of correct cutting and finishing. The installation routines detailed below will ensure that the shift mechanism is primed. Both Shimano and Campagnolo systems use a ratchet system to turn a winding wheel, which pulls a calibrated length of cable. The mechanism for front and rear levers is a mirror image. Shimano's STI shift mechanism sits in the lever itself and is recognizable by the outer casing running from the top of the lever, while the Campagnolo design is positioned within the lever body, allowing the outer casing to exit against the handlebar.

Installation of Shimano dual-function lever cables

Time: 20 minutes
Grade of job: moderate
Tools: small screwdriver, cable cutter

Note that the brake and primary shift levers are combined in one unit. Behind the primary lever sits a smaller lever; this shifts the chain to a smaller sprocket or chainring, while the primary lever shifts it to a larger sprocket or chainring. If both levers are pressed at once, no shift will take place.

1 Start by pushing the secondary lever inwards several times. Pull the brake lever back to reveal the top of the mechanism. The winding wheel will be visible. On it can be seen the stop for the inner-wire nipple.

2 As the secondary lever is depressed, the stop will move inwards across the top of the lever.

3 Thread the tip of the inner wire through the hole from the outside of the lever, so that it exits through the locating hole for the outer casing. If the angle between the two parts is too great, simultaneously depress the secondary lever and push the winding wheel inwards with the tip of a screwdriver. It will click home.

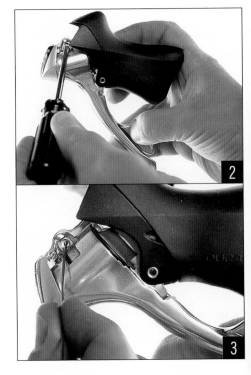

4 Install the outer casing and inner wire, and pull on the inner wire while again depressing the secondary lever several times. When the winding wheel is fully seated, begin derailleur installation as described on page 66.

Installation of Campagnolo dual-function lever cables

Time: 20 minutes
Grade of job: moderate
Tools: small screwdriver, cable cutters

Note that the primary shift lever sits behind the brake lever, and shifts the chain to a larger sprocket or chainring. The secondary lever is positioned on the inside of the lever housing, and it shifts the chain to a smaller sprocket or chainring.

1 Look on the underside of the Ergo Power lever. There is a slot in the rubber hood, and inside this slot sits the winding wheel. The stop for the inner wire must be to the outside of the lever body before the wire is installed. Depress the secondary lever several times; this should move the stop around to the outside. If not, assist by pushing it with the tip of a screwdriver while depressing the lever.

2 Next, install the lever assembly as described on page 42.

3 Thread the inner wire upward through the stop on the winding wheel and then the lever body. It will emerge from the top of the body.

4 Push it through the outer casing (with ferrule) and then push the outer casing firmly into the lever body. Proceed with derailleur installation as described on page 66.

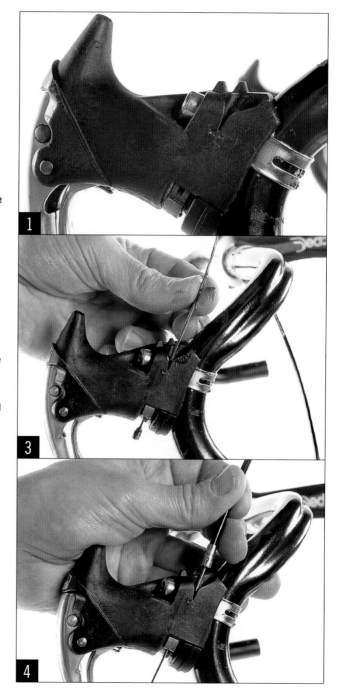

SRAM Gripshift cables

Gripshift is a system that integrates the shifting mechanism with the handlebar grips on flat handlebars only. It works with SRAM or Shimano nine-speed derailleur systems and is popular with recreational cyclists and mountain bikers, since it allows them to keep their grip on the bars at all times. The rider simply turns the inner barrel to change gear, and each shift is accompanied by a tangible click. There have been a number of improvements to Gripshift since it was launched, but the principle is as described here.

Installation of SRAM Gripshift cables

Time: 20 minutes
Grade of job: moderate
Tools: Allen keys, cable cutters

1 Remove the outer grips with a long screwdriver. If this proves difficult, apply spray lube using a tube nozzle to ease removal.

2 Remove the cable retaining plate, and then unship and remove the special Gripshift 1.1mm inner wire.

3 Slacken the clamping screw (slot head in earlier versions) and slide the housing off the bars.

4 Clean the mechanism thoroughly with washing-up liquid, shampoo or similar. Once clean and dry, coat all surfaces (except the handlebar mating surface) with silicon lube before refitting and clamping the housing.

5 Replace the inner wire in the retaining plate, and refit the plate after threading the inner wire though the housing adjuster. Coat the inside with rubber solution or spray with hairspray and replace the grips. Then replace the outer casing and install the derailleur mechanisms as described on page 66. Adjust the gears using the barrel adjuster.

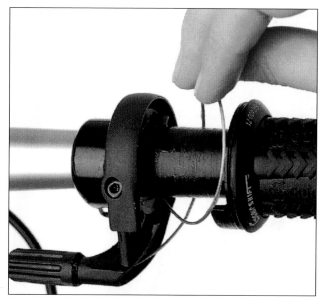

Some Gripshifts require the cable to be looped around the barrel of the unit.

5

Downtube levers

Before the introduction of dual-control levers, gear shifters were usually sited on the downtube of the frame. The latest downtube levers are indexed, making shifting straightforward, but earlier levers had simple friction mechanisms inside. There are too many different internal mechanisms to show, so if servicing an existing set of levers, note carefully the order of disassembly. The general principle is demonstrated here using a pair of Shimano indexed nine-speed levers.

Fitting downtube levers

Time: 15 minutes
Grade of job: easy
Tools: screwdriver

The frame is already fitted with shaped bosses containing integral threads. These should be tapped out on new steel frames.

1 Install the first spacer, noting that the dog on the lever side must face forwards.

2 Turn the lever so that the nipple housing faces up and the lever forwards; align the spacer on the inside of the lever with the dog on the spacer, and push the lever onto the boss.

3 Install the screw and tighten it enough to secure the lever without jamming. Friction levers should be tightened enough to keep them positioned against the tension on the derailleur cable. The Shimano model illustrated can be switched from friction to indexed operation using the ring handle.

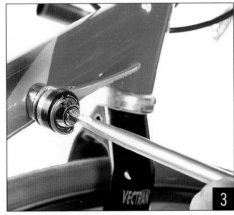

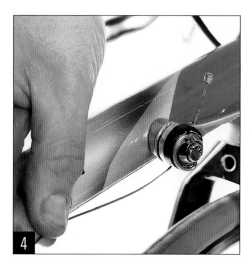

4 The inner wire on all downtube levers is threaded through from the top and curved round the underside. A groove is provided to retain the inner wire. The lever must be pushed fully forwards before beginning rear-derailleur installation.

5 The left-hand lever has the same first spacer, which must be installed with the dog facing forwards. Install the lever body so that it engages with the spacer, and then fit the securing screw.

6 Before fully tightening the screw, turn the lever anti-clockwise against its stop.

7 Then, turn the screw enough to keep the lever in place against its own internal spring.

8 Fit the inner wire and adjust the front mech as described on page 66.

Identify your crankset

The crankset comprises both cranks and their chainrings, which are sometimes called chainwheels. The number of gears on a cycle with derailleur gears is calculated by multiplying the number of sprockets on the rear wheel by the number of chainrings. Triple chainrings are usually found on touring and mountain bikes, and are ideal where extra-low gears are required. Double chainrings, which are lighter than triple chainrings, provide a sufficient range of gears for racing and most sports riding. A single chainring is usually found on utility cycles with hub gears, and on fixed-wheel machines ridden on a banked track or velodrome.

Triple
The innermost chainring provides additional extra-low gears.

Double

Double chainrings are usual for racing.

Single

Favoured on utility cycles and for use on the velodrome.

Cartridge bottom brackets

The cranks rotate on a bearing contained within the bottom bracket of the frame. This is the most heavily stressed bearing on the cycle and, therefore, the most substantially constructed. The most common type of bottom bracket in current use is made as a complete, sealed unit that is not user-serviceable. Installation requires a specially shaped tool specific to the cartridge type; the Shimano axle shown requires a splined tool.

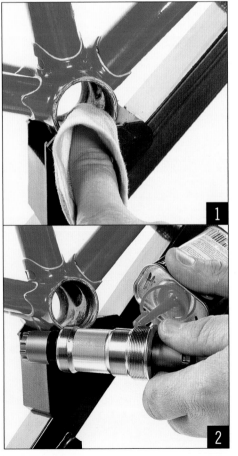

Installing a cartridge bottom bracket

Time: 15 minutes
Grade of job: moderate
Tools: splined tool, lubricating oil, spanner or torque wrench, cleaning materials

1 Clean the thread inside the bottom-bracket shell. An old toothbrush will get into the threads; first spray them with a light lube or solvent to soften any old grease. The threads in a new frame should be tapped out and the shell faced; this job should be carried out by a cycle shop.

2 Oil the threads on the body of the cartridge, and thread it into the right-hand side of the bracket shell. The first three turns should be made by hand to avoid the risk of cross-threading. Frames with a British thread will have a left-hand thread on this side, so the assembly will have to be turned anti-clockwise. Italian frames (with the exception of Bianchi) have a right-hand thread on both sides of the bracket shell. Take a close look at the thread before installing the cartridge.

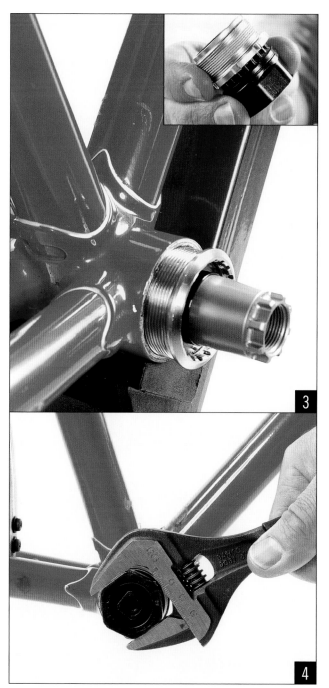

3 When the cartridge is halfway installed, thread the left-hand cup part way into the bracket shell. If it has a locking compound applied, do not oil the threads (see inset).

4 Now finish tightening the cartridge body. If a torque wrench is available, tighten to about 50Nm, otherwise, apply considerable force with a lever about 300mm (12in) long.

5 Finish tightening the left-hand cup. This is usually made in a plastic resin or in light alloy, so avoid using excessive force. Turn the axle by hand to ensure that the bearings are not binding.

To remove a cartridge assembly, perform the five steps in reverse sequence but remove the left-hand cup completely before unscrewing the cartridge, and confirm whether the frame has left- or right-hand threads before attempting to unscrew the cartridge. When attempting to loosen either side, ensure that your hands will not be injured should the splined tool or spanner slip.

Square-taper cranks

The majority of cranksets are attached to a bottom-bracket axle that has four flats on its end. The axle's shape matches flats on the inside of the crank, which are tapered to provide a secure fit.

Removal of square-taper cranks

Time: 15 minutes
Grade of job: moderate
Tools: crank extractor, spanner, Allen key

Cranks may be fitted with a self-extractor bolt – which is recognizable by a ring – fitted in the crank thread, around the head of the crankbolt. To remove, simply unscrew the crankbolt, which bears against the inside of the ring and pushes the crank off the axle.

1 If the bolt is not of this type, remove the crank dust cap and crankbolt.

2 Back off the thread in the extractor tool, and thread it fully into the crank.

3 Tighten the body of the tool with a spanner.

4 Tighten the extractor centre bolt until it bears against the end of the axle. Now, use a spanner to turn it further; this will require some force initially, but once the crank loosens it can be pulled off the axle. Remove the extractor.

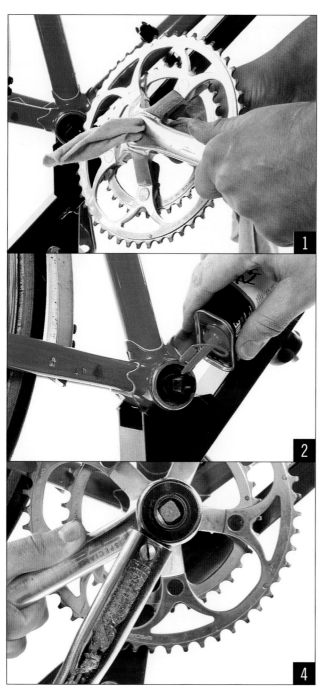

Installation of square-taper cranks

Time: 15 minutes
Grade of job: moderate
Tools: light oil, Allen key or socket spanner, torque wrench

1 All mating surfaces should be cleaned thoroughly before installation. Pull a clean rag through the hole in the crank.

2 Oil the axle flats. Position the crank over the axle, and push it into place by hand. If a self-extractor bolt is fitted, this must be turned at the same time.

3 If separate, install the crankbolt, and tighten it by hand until resistance is felt.

4 Using a long Allen key or torque wrench with socket (shown), tighten the crank on to the axle. Do not use excessive force, since square-taper cranks can be damaged if over tightened. Apply about 40Nm or moderate force with a 200mm Allen key. Fit a dust cap if the crank thread is exposed.

Octalink-splined cranks

Octalink is the name for an axle and crank connection used by Shimano. It may be recognized by the eight small splines on each end of the axle, and by matching lobes on the inside of the crank. The removal process is as for square-taper cranks. However, if removing a crank without a self-extractor bolt, fit the special Shimano adaptor piece before using the extractor tool. Care is required during installation to ensure that the splines are properly engaged. If the splines are not engaged correctly, severe damage may result.

Installation of Octalink-splined cranks

Time: 15 minutes
Grade of job: moderate
Tools: grease, Allen key, cleaning materials

1 Clean all old grease from the end of the axle and from the smooth round surface on the inside of the crank.

2 If self-extractor bolts are fitted, align the splines of the first crank and axle as far as possible.

3 Turn the crankbolt using an Allen key until the thread engages. Continue turning the bolt until resistance is felt. The tips of the splines are now touching the axle.

4 Hold the other end of the axle and wiggle it inside the crank; it should be possible to feel the point at which the splines are aligned. Tighten the bolt one turn.

5 Repeat the process with the second crank. Ensure that the two are aligned at 180 degrees.

6 At this stage, if both cranks are correctly installed, there will be a minute amount of play as they are pulled back and forth.

7 Once certain that the lobes in each crank are located correctly between the axle splines, fully tighten each crank in turn. The Octalink system requires more force than the square taper design; apply enough force to a 200mm Allen key to seat each crank fully. Once seated, the resistance of the Allen key will suddenly increase.

Cottered cranksets

Although now obsolete, many older cycles still use cottered cranksets. The cottered crank is secured to its axle using a cotter pin, which runs through the crank and the axle. Pins come in either metric or imperial sizes, and unfilled cotters are also available.

Axle flat

Cotter pin

Nut

Removing a cottered crankset

Time: 10 minutes   **Grade of job:** moderate   **Equipment:** peg spanner, hammer

1 Unscrew the nut on the cotter pin until its top is flush with the end of the thread. Support the underside of the crank with a block of wood so that the crank does not bear on the axle. Loosen the cotter pin by hammering the nut. Remove the nut, and use a drift to drive the pin through the crank.

2 A new cotter pin must be filed to size before fitting. The thread is offset from the centre, and a flat must be filed on the side opposite the pin. Where a flat has already been machined, the pin should be tried for size before further filing. Both pins must be filed to the same angle, and both must face the same way (i.e. in or against the direction of rotation).

3 When pushed through the crank, enough thread for the nut and washer should be visible. If the pin pushes through too far, preventing the nut from being tightened, discard the pin. Before tightening the nut, give the other end of the pin several smart taps with a hammer to seat it.

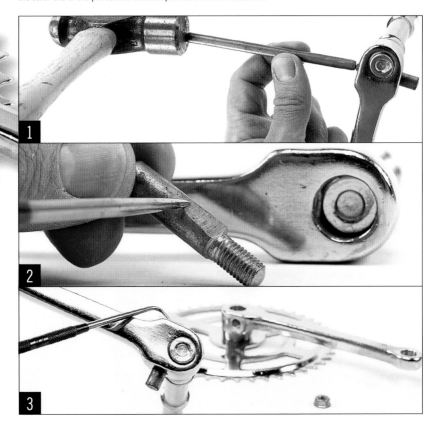

Chainrings

Chainrings should be maintained in good condition to ensure that the transmission works efficiently. Potential problems include excessive tooth wear, bent or missing teeth and warping of the complete ring. Wear is excessive when the forward and backward faces of the tooth are no longer symmetrical. The tip of the forward face will normally wear away first. Some chainrings made by the French company TA have asymmetrical teeth; have these inspected by a mechanic if unsure of their condition. Other chainrings are designed with teeth partially missing to improve shifting; broken teeth can be recognized by a jagged edge. Bent teeth should be straightened with care, as light alloy teeth easily snap. A warped chainring will show against the front-derailleur plates. A minor warp may be corrected using an adjustable spanner. Chainrings can be exchanged to alter overall gear ratios, but doing so may necessitate a change in chain length.

Installation of chainrings

Time: 20 minutes
Grade of job: moderate
Tools: Allen key, peg spanner

1 Decide how many chainrings need to be secured by the bolts being fitted. Separate screws usually secure the inner ring of a triple chainset. For a double chainset, position both chainrings on the arms of the crank spider. Ensure that both rings face the correct way – with the inset on the bolt holes facing away from the spider arms – and that the peg on the big ring is behind the crank.

2 Install the first nut in the inner ring. This nut will also locate the outer ring.

3 Oil the threads of the chainring bolt and screw it into the nut. Do not tighten it fully.

4 Repeat with the remaining nuts and bolts.

5 Once all bolts are in place, tighten them using an Allen key and a peg spanner. Tighten the first bolt, then the bolt two away and so on to avoid warping the rings. Always run around the chainring bolts on a new bicycle with an Allen key.

Identify your derailleur

Derailleur gear shifting mechanisms do just that; they derail the chain from one sprocket or chainring to another. The pedals must be turning for a shift to take place. The system is preferred for all but utility cycles because it is light and efficient, and offers a large number of gear ratios.

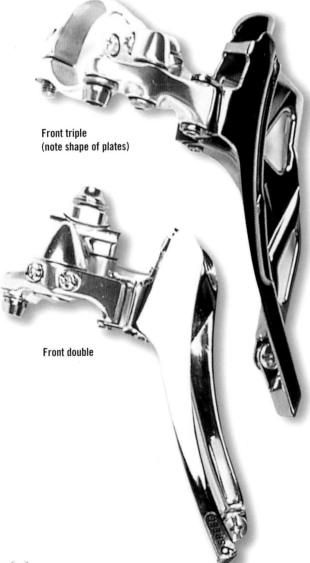

**Front triple
(note shape of plates)**

Front double

The front mech

The front mech is designed solely to shift the chain between chainrings. However, the shape of the cage plates differs according to the number of rings. A triple front mech will work with a double chainset, but not vice versa. Front mechs are either clamped around the frame seat tube or attached to a special lug.

To guarantee optimal shifting performance, always combine transmission components as intended by the manufacturer.

The rear mech

The rear mech has to perform two functions: firstly, it must shift the chain across the rear sprockets; and, secondly, it must keep the chain in tension. Rear mechs for triple chainsets need a longer cage for the jockey wheels, as they must be able to take up the extra chain slack left by the gap between the largest and smallest chainrings. Triple rear mechs will work with double chainrings, but not vice versa. Mountain bike rear mechs operate over a steeper angle than those used on road bikes to accommodate wide ratio sprockets.

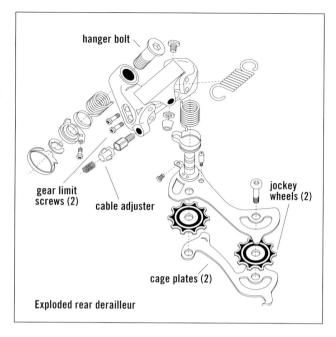

hanger bolt

gear limit screws (2)

cable adjuster

jockey wheels (2)

cage plates (2)

Exploded rear derailleur

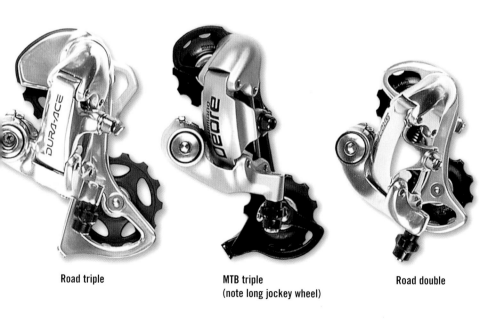

Road triple

MTB triple (note long jockey wheel)

Road double

Rear mech

The rear mech and its accompanying shifter form the most complex mechanism on the cycle. Accurate and reliable shifting depends on precise adjustment of the mech, and this should be done both during installation and at any time that shift quality deteriorates. Indexed systems shift one gear per click, and once set up they require little skill to operate. The now-obsolete friction systems only require throw adjustment, but they are harder to operate. The following instructions are for an indexed rear mech.

Rear mech installation and adjustment

Time: 30 minutes
Grade of job: difficult
Tools: Allen keys, cable cutter, small screwdriver, pliers, grease, ruler

1 Start by greasing the thread on the mech's upper-pivot bolt. The thread in the dropout gear hanger must be clean and free from debris. Ask a bike-shop mechanic to tap it out if necessary. Thread the pivot bolt into the hanger, ensuring that the small adjuster screw does not jam against the side of the hanger. Once tight, check that the mech pivots freely.

2 Check that the two jockey wheels and any sprocket are perfectly parallel. If the jockey wheels are at an angle to the sprocket, the gear hanger is bent and shifting will be poor. Ask a bike shop to straighten it.

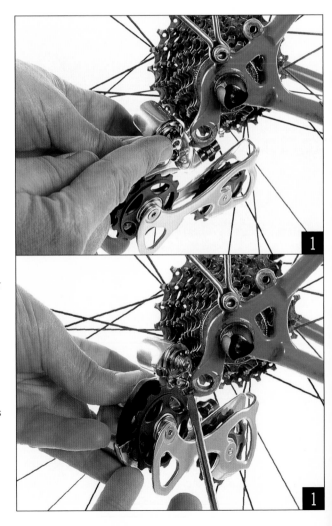

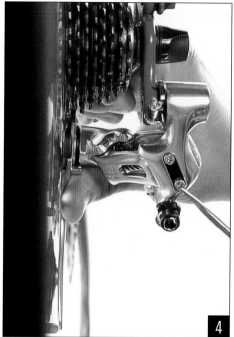

3 Use the appropriate throw-adjuster screw (upper on Shimano mechs) to align the jockey wheels with the smallest sprocket. The screws are on the outer side plate on Campagnolo mechs.

4 Push the jockey-wheel cage across to the inside, and use the other throw-adjuster screw to allow the wheels to align roughly with the largest sprocket.

5 Turn the cable adjuster until it is about halfway along its range. Install the gear cable as described on page 23, and tighten the inner wire clamp.

6 Hold the rear mech with one hand, and pull hard on the inner wire where it runs beside the downtube. This will seat the outer casings.

7 If the inner wire is now slack, loosen the clamp, pull the wire through with pliers and retighten the clamp.

8 Move the primary shift lever one click. This should move the rear mech slightly. If not, repeat step 6 until excess slack is removed from the system.

9 Install the chain as described on page 76.

10 With the chain on the smallest sprocket, use the small screw behind the gear hanger to move the upper jockey wheel until it is as close to the sprocket as possible without touching it.

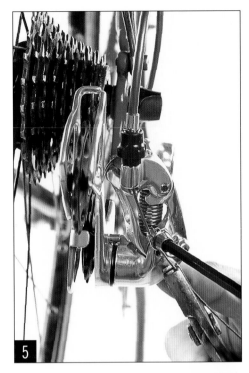

5

6

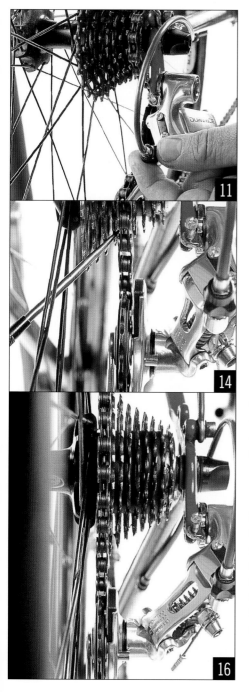

11 Press the secondary shift lever to ensure that the winding wheel (see page 44) is at its start point. Press the primary shift lever one click; the chain should climb on to the second sprocket. If it shifts too far, turn the cable adjuster inward half a turn. If not far enough, turn it out by one turn.

12 Shift back on to the small sprocket. If the chain will not return, slacken the throw-adjuster screw half a turn. Repeat step 10.

13 When the chain will shift happily between the first two sprockets, shift it to the middle sprocket, or either middle sprocket if there is an even number.

14 Use the cable adjuster to align the chain precisely with the centre-line of the sprocket.

15 Shift the chain one sprocket in each direction. If it shifts more easily to a smaller sprocket, bias the mech slightly by turning the adjuster one quarter-turn out, and vice versa.

16 Shift the mech across to the largest sprocket. If the chain will not climb on to the sprocket, slacken the throw adjuster until it does. If the chain moves too far, turn the adjuster inwards. Repeat the process until the chain moves easily on to the largest sprocket without trying to climb off it.

17 Shift through all the sprockets, checking that the jockey wheel does not touch the sprocket. If so, use the small screw behind the hanger to move it away from the sprocket. Shift on to the other chainrings and repeat the shifts. If the chain shifts poorly on any sprocket, make adjustments with the chain on the middle sprocket. If these adjustments fail to correct poor shifting, check for corroded or kinked control cables, a bent gear hanger, seized jockey wheels, a stiff chain link or worn rear mech, and replace as necessary.

Front mech

Front mechs work by pushing against the side plates of the chain to move it from one ring to another. Front mechs rely heavily on the shape and alignment of their cage plates. Once the chain has shifted, it may touch one of the cage plates depending on the rear sprocket selected. To prevent this the cage plates must be carefully aligned. Furthermore, the shift lever allows some 'trimming' of cage position. Unlike the rear mech, successful front-mech adjustment depends to some extent on practised judgement, and it may be necessary, when setting up, to experiment until the ideal alignment is found. The process is the same for triple chainsets. Use the inner and outer chainrings to set up the front mech.

Installation and adjustment

Time: 15 minutes
Grade of job: difficult
Tools: Allen keys, small screwdriver

1 Start by clamping the mech lightly to the seat tube. Undo the small screw at the tip of the cage plates and spread them to clear the chain if it is already in place. New mechs will contain a plastic peg, which must be left in place until step 3.

2 The plastic peg keeps the cage roughly over the outside chainring. If it is missing, use the inner throw adjuster to position the outer cage plate over the ring.

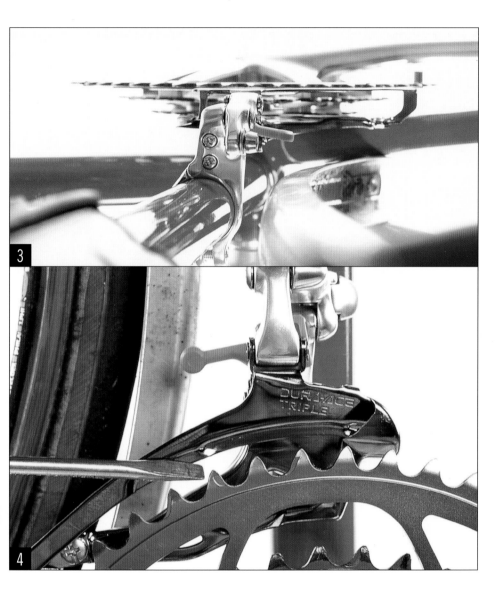

3 Align the outer plate parallel to the centre-line of the
outer chainring; this adjustment must be precise.

4 Move the mech up or down until the underside of the outer
plate is about 2mm (1/16in) above the top of the chainring
teeth. Rotate the crank one turn to make sure that no teeth are
closer than 2mm (1/16in) to the cage plate.

5 If not already fitted, install the chain as described on page 76.

6 Place the chain on the inner chainring and largest sprocket, and use the appropriate throw adjuster to shift the cage plates until they clear the chain equally on both sides.

7 Make sure the shift lever is in the start position, and install the cable inner wire.

8 Position the downtube cable adjuster halfway along its range before clamping. Pull hard on the inner wire to seat the casings, and repeat the process to remove any slack in the wire.

9 Shift the rear mech to the smallest sprocket.

10 Turning the pedals, pull gently on the inner wire to move the chain on to the largest chainring. If it fails to climb on to the ring, slacken the appropriate throw screw. If it looks likely to throw the chain off the outside of the ring, hold the mech in place with the wire and adjust the throw screw accordingly.

11 Turn the pedals and pull on the wire repeatedly to shift the chain between the inner and outer chainrings. Make further throw adjustments as needed until the chain shifts cleanly and without any tendency to climb off a ring.

12 Now use the shift lever to move the chain on to the big ring. Push the primary lever hard over; when it is released, the front mech should not move at all. If it moves even slightly inwards, move the cable adjuster outwards to take up any slack.

13 It should now be possible to press lightly on the secondary lever and find a soft click. This will trim the cage inwards by a small amount.

14 Shift the rear mech to the sixth or seventh sprocket. If the cage outer plate touches the side of the chain, add more tension to the cable casing using the adjuster. If the inner plate touches the chain, slacken the adjuster by one-quarter of a turn. The object is to be able to trim the mech to miss the chain whether it is on the smaller or larger sprockets.

15 Sometimes it is not possible to correct the cage trim using cable adjustment alone. If the chain shows a tendency to rub on the outer cage plate, the front mech may be turned so that the cage is slightly 'tail out' by a maximum of 3mm (⅛in).

16 When satisfied with the trim, again pull on the inner wire to shift the chain across the rings. Turn the pedals fast and shift the chain rapidly back and forth, moving it into each rear sprocket at least twice to ensure that the chain does not jump off when shifting on the road.

Identify your chain

The drive chain on all modern bicycles is a roller chain, with paired side plates joined by pins. These are press-fitted into the outer plates, and run freely through the inner plates. Each pin has a roller around it that runs smoothly on to the teeth of the chainwheels and reduces friction.

The standard pitch, or distance, between pins, is ½in, but bicycle chains are made in a variety of widths. Utility machines are usually fitted with a ⅛in chain. Cycles equipped with derailleur gears have chains that are nominally ³⁄₃₂in, although there are a number of variations in width dependent on the number of rear sprockets.

The finish applied to the chain may be anything from full nickel plating to nothing; non-plated chains corrode very quickly. A selection of joining methods is employed, from the traditional split link found on ⅛in chains to Campagnolo's Perma-Link connector. Most chains are now supplied with a connecting link, which invariably ensures the safest and most reliable join.

Shimano HG with joining pin.
For use with derailleur transmission.

SRAM derailleur chain with Powerlink.
Gold link is used with 9-speed chain.

1⅛ in utility chain with split link.

Wipperman derailleur chain with Connex connector.
Note different slot shape compared to SRAM Powerlink.

Chain inspection

A well-maintained roller chain transmission is very efficient, but it will deteriorate rapidly as soon as any part begins to wear noticeably. Sprocket teeth only wear out when run with a stretched chain, so chains should be replaced frequently to preserve sprocket life.

The rule of thumb for chain wear is to replace when the chain has stretched by one per cent. There are various ways to measure stretch, but if no tool is available the chain should be measured using a ruler as follows:

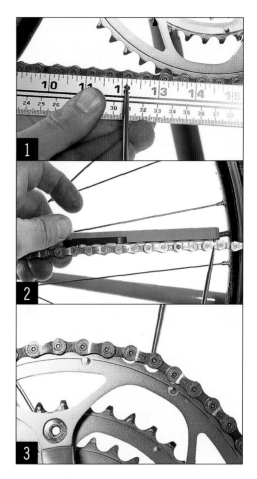

1 Measure across 24 pins. Taking the example of a standard chain, with pins spaced at ½in intervals, this measurement should be 12in. Multiply 12in by one per cent and you get ⅛in. If the chain measures 12⅛in over 24 links, it should be replaced.

2 Tools such as the Park Chainchecker provide a quick and highly accurate reading of chain wear.

3 An alternative quick-check is to pull the chain away from the front of the big chainring; if more than two-thirds of a tooth is visible, the chain is excessively worn.

Chain lubrication

Time: 5 minutes
Grade of job: easy
Tools: chain lube, cleaning materials

Ideally, the chain should be cleaned as described on page 24 before being lubed. The best way to keep a chain well lubed and clean is to apply a little oil to each link individually, allowing it to run inside the roller and between the side plates. Spraying the chain with lube as it is turned is quick and easy, but messy and wasteful.

Derailleur type

Derailleur transmissions rely on spare chain to accommodate the different sizes of the various chainring and sprocket combinations. When installing a derailleur chain, allowance must be made for the range of gears without exceeding the capacity of the rear mech. The chain must also be joined, and each of the major chain manufacturers employs a different proprietary connecting link. These should be used for a safe, quick join, but where no connecting link is available, the chain can usually be joined by the traditional method described on page 78.

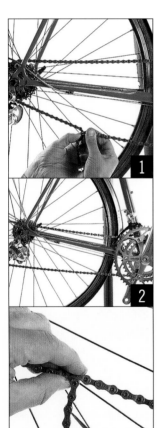

Determining chain length

There are two main methods of determining correct chain length.

1 The method recommended by manufacturers is to run the chain on the largest sprocket and chainring, and exclude the rear mech. Let one end of the chain overlap the other, and add two links to the first link that overlaps. Break the chain here. If fitting a chain with a separate connecting link, only add one link before breaking the chain.

2 The alternative method leaves a longer chain and puts less tension into the rear mech. Put the cycle in the second smallest sprocket and smallest chainring, wrapping the chain around the rear mech.

3 Now pull the ends of the chain together and overlap them until the lower run of the chain no longer rubs on the jockey wheel cage above. Break the chain to leave the longest possible length that does not rub.

The SRAM Powerlink

This simple link comprises two identical pieces assembled asymmetrically. The chain must be cut to leave an inner link at each end. Push the pin of each piece through the exposed hole. Pull the ends of the chain together, and push the pins through their opposing holes in the Powerlink plates (bottom). Make sure that the pins are snug in their grooves, and pull the ends apart. Bend the chain sideways, and the pins will be seated (top).

Installation of connecting links

Time: 15 minutes
Grade of job: moderate
Tools: chain tool suitable for chain type

Shimano

1 New Shimano chains are supplied with a single-use pin already in place in one side plate. The chain should be cut to length, and the pin simply driven through the inner link into the opposing side plate. The pin has locating ridges that snap tangibly into the side plate.

2 If the chain is to be broken and rejoined, a new pin of the correct type must be used. Do not break chain at original pin. Eight- and nine-speed chains use special pins that have two parts divided by a narrow waist. The ends of the chain are aligned and the conical tip of one end is pushed through the holes.

3 Once the guide end has passed through, the pin itself is driven through until the securing ridges are felt to snap into place. The guide tip is then broken off.

4 Flex the chain sideways to loosen the join.

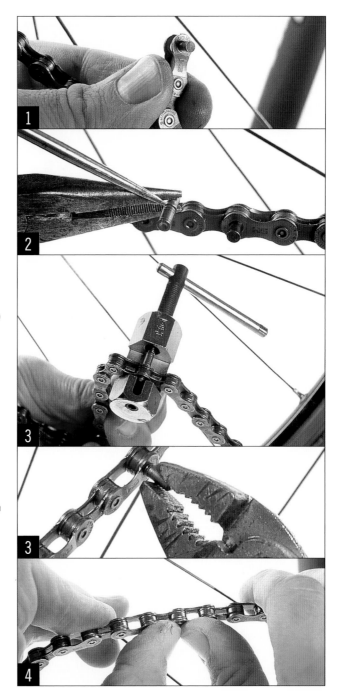

Campagnolo

Campagnolo ten-speed chains must be joined using the special Perma-Link. This operation requires a dedicated straight-push cramp, and should be performed by a trained mechanic.

1 The chain is cut to leave inner links at the end. These are pushed over the side plate with pins, and the other side plate put in place.

2 A small rivet is placed in each Perma-Link pin, and driven into place using the cramp. The jaws must be set to 4mm before driving the rivets.

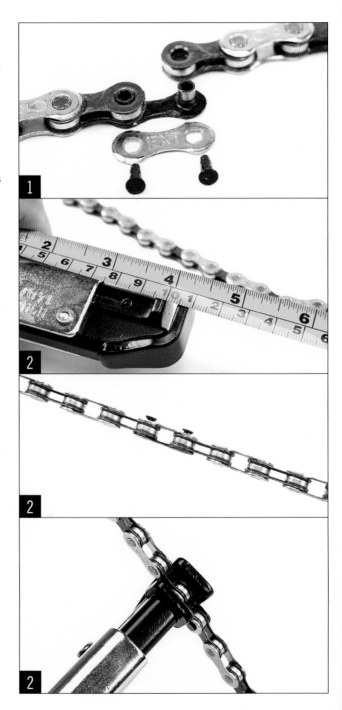

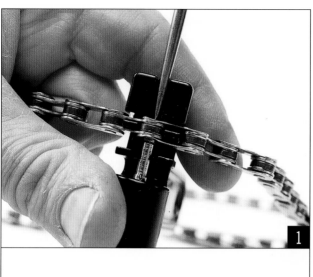

The traditional method

1 The traditional method of joining a derailleur chain is to use a chain tool to push a pin most of the way through the opposite outer plate. Leave about 1mm (1⁄20in) of the pin proud of the inside of the plate.

2 Now snap the outer link with pin into place over the inner link. The projecting end of the pin acts as a guide and keeps the chain positioned for the next stage.

3 Use the tool to drive the pin through the inner link and into the opposing outer plate until the tip projects by the same amount as the tips of the pins on either side.

4 The chain will now have a stiff link. Turn the tool around and back off the driving pin. The link can now be positioned on the rear set pegs. Drive the pin back into the link slightly. The pin will move but the plate will stay put, loosening the link. This cannot be done with a Shimano HG chain tool.

Utility type chain

Utility and track bikes are fitted with a ⅛in chain, which is hard wearing but unsuitable for use with derailleur gears. This type of chain is usually joined with a split link, which is kept closed by a spring-clip.

Installation and slack adjustment

Time: 15 minutes
Grade of job: moderate
Tools: chain tool, pliers, axle-nut spanners

1 Place the rear wheel about halfway along the frame dropouts and lightly tighten the nuts or QR lever.

2 Place the chain over the chainring and sprocket, and pull the ends together. Note the gap between the inner link at one end and the inner link nearest it when the chain is pulled taut; this will either be slightly more or slightly less than the ⅛in pitch of the split link. Break the chain at this point.

3 Slacken the axle nuts and shift the wheel forwards in the dropout to bring the ends of the chain readily together. Install the split-link side plate with pins, and then the second plate; this will leave the ends of the pin proud.

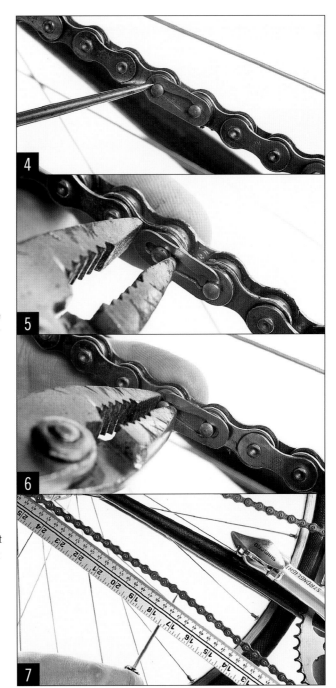

4 Push the spring-clip into place. The end of the clip must always trail, or face away from the direction of chain travel.

5 Install the clip by placing the ends up against the groove in the end of the pin, and then use pliers to grip the back of the clip and the near pin. Close the pliers to snap the clip into place.

6 To remove a ⅛in chain, follow the above procedure in reverse.

7 Adjust the rear wheel to leave about ½in (12mm) of slack at the tightest point.

Identify your freewhee

The earliest multiple freewheels, colloquially called 'blocks', were simply a development of the basic single-freewheel, which screws directly on to the hub and keeps the freewheel mechanism within the block itself. The design, which was eventually developed to accommodate a total of eight sprockets, is still used today in low-cost cycles. For most purposes it has been superseded by the freehub, which places the freewheel mechanism within the hub. Besides being easy to assemble and lightweight, freehubs are durable and need little maintenance.

The sprockets are mounted on a freehub body and are retained by a single lock-ring. The sprockets are described collectively as the 'cassette', which may contain between seven and ten sprockets. They may be installed individually or as a complete cassette, and a block is easily distinguished from a cassette by the splines on the inside of the latter.

Shimano freehub

Campagnolo 9/10-speed freehub

Mountain bike
cassette
(front)

Threaded
'block'
(front)

Shimano 9-speed
cassette
(front)

Campagnolo
8-speed cassette
(front)

Mountain bike
cassette
(back)

Threaded
'block'
(back)

Shimano 9-speed
cassette
(back)

Campagnolo
8-speed cassette
(back)

Cassette freewheels

There are currently two formats for the splines on freehub bodies. Shimano's pattern is the same as that used for mountain bikes, and is the most commonly used; while the current Campagnolo spline pattern can accept eight-, nine- and ten-speed cassettes. The two formats are not interchangeable, but the same principle applies to both.

Installation of cassette

Time: 10 minutes
Grade of job: moderate
Tools: splined lock-ring tool, spanner

1 Sort the sprockets into size order if separate, ensuring that any markings face outwards. Remove the wheel's QR skewer. Turn the freehub body until the narrow spline (Shimano) or stepped spline (Campagnolo) is uppermost.

2 Align the first sprocket with the freehub body and push it on. Each of the two formats has a particular spline pattern, which only allows the sprockets to be mounted in one position. This ensures that shifting ramps machined into the sprocket faces are effective.

3 Fit a spacer if necessary. Note the order of sprockets and spacers when removing a cassette, and repeat when installing the sprockets. If fitting a new cassette, observe the assembly order described in the literature.

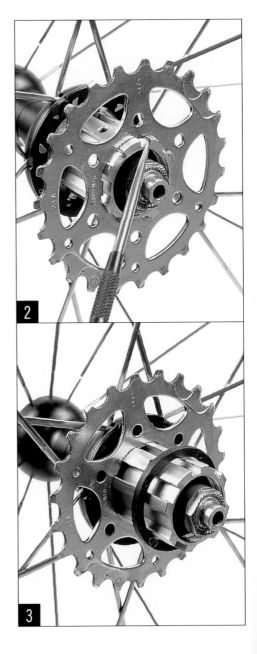

Removal of cassette

Time: 5 minutes
Grade of job: easy
Tools: splined tool, chain wrench, spanner

1 Fit the chain wrench to the largest sprocket to prevent the cassette from turning.

2 Fit the lock-ring tool, and unscrew anti-clockwise.

3 Remove the cassette.

4 Fit the next sprocket. All markings must face outwards. To make assembly easier the markings on successive sprockets will all line up.

5 Repeat the process until all sprockets are in place. Fit the threaded lock-ring and tighten it with moderate force.

Threaded freewheels

The freewheel mechanism of a threaded block is vulnerable to the effects of water, grit and other corrosive elements. It should be checked after every ride in poor weather for rough running and signs of deterioration. The easiest way to strip a block is to leave it screwed to the hub so that it is held steady while the lock-ring is removed.

Maintenance of threaded-type freewheel

Time: 15 minutes
Grade of job: moderate
Tools: centre-punch, hammer, grease

1 Remove the QR skewer if fitted.

2 Locate one of the small holes in the outer bearing plate. Position the end of the centre-punch in the hole, align it at a suitable angle, and use the hammer to drive the bearing plate in a clockwise direction. Wear eye protection.

3 Remove the bearing plate to reveal the balls and spring pawls. Collect any thin shims.

4 Pull the sprockets off the hub, taking care to catch any balls and small parts that fall out.

5 Clean all parts thoroughly, grease the races and reposition the balls and spring pawls.

6 Refit the sprocket body. To pass it over the pawls, turn it anti-clockwise while pushing it into place. Try turning it clockwise to check that the pawls engage.

7 Refit the outer plate, with shims if found. Tighten the plate using the hammer and centre-punch.

Fitment of threaded-type freewheels

Time: 5 minutes
Grade of job: easy
Tools: wheel and freewheel

1 Oil the threads on the hub.

2 Carefully engage the freewheel threads with the hub, and screw them into place by hand. If the fit is too tight, remove the freewheel and try again.

3 Fit the rear wheel, shift the chain to a suitable gear and **gently** apply pedalling force to tighten the block. Riding the bike will complete the process.

Removal of threaded-type freewheels

Time: 5 minutes
Grade of job: moderate
Tools: suitable removal tool, vice, QR skewer

1 Place the removal tool in the vice.

2 Remove the QR skewer and place the wheel – freewheel side down – over the removal tool.

3 Ensure that the splines (or 'dogs') of the removal tool are engaged. Grip the wheel rim and turn it sharply anti-clockwise (as viewed from above).

4 If the tool feels like it may slip, secure it to the wheel with the QR skewer and a couple of large washers. Remove the skewer once the block has loosened.

Identify your pedals

Clipless pedals have had as great an impact on cycling comfort and efficiency as indexed gear shifting. All clipless pedals work by capturing a shaped cleat, which is fixed on the underside of the shoe, in a mechanical trap. The jaws of the trap are shaped to release the cleat when it is twisted sideways. To get into the pedal, the foot must be pressed downwards until it engages. To release the shoe, the foot is simply turned heel out, ideally at the bottom of the pedal stroke. Double-sided pedals are used on mountain bikes for rapid entry. The large, protruding cleats used on competition road shoes make walking difficult; mountain-bike shoes allow easy walking and are better for touring and commuting. There are numerous pedal, cleat and shoe formats. Some shoes will accept several cleat types, often by using a sole-adaptor. If in doubt, ask a shop for advice.

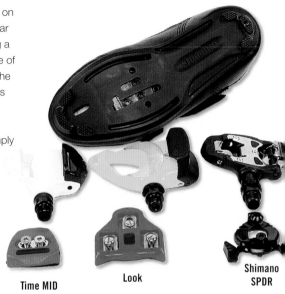

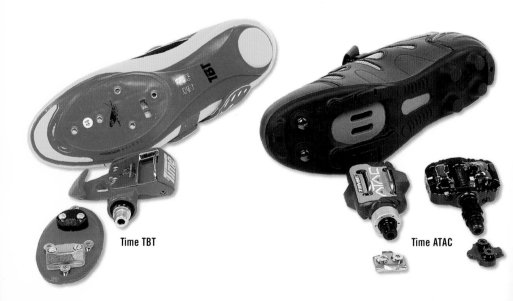

Time MID

Look

Shimano SPDR

Time TBT

Time ATAC

Replacing pedals

Time: 10 minutes
Grade of job: easy
Tools: pedal spanner, pedal
washers, grease, clean rag

1 Before fitting a pedal, grease the
thread and wipe any dirt away from
the thread in the crank. If the axle flats
run up to the crank, use pedal washers
to prevent scoring.

2 Start the thread using fingers for at
least one turn to avoid cross-
threading, and then fit the spanner.

3 Holding the spanner with one hand,
rotate the pedal and crank rapidly
backwards with the other hand until you
feel resistance. Then tighten the axle
against the crank with the spanner
using moderate force.

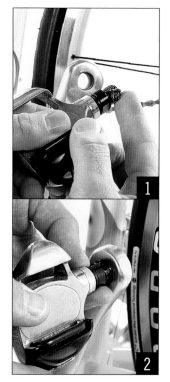

Removing pedals

When removing or fitting pedals, remember that
the left-hand pedal has a left-hand thread, which
means that it tightens anti-clockwise. The right-
hand pedal has a normal, clockwise thread.
Pedals use a standard thread size, making
replacement straightforward.

Always use a pedal spanner for removal or
fitment of pedals; its narrow jaws fit the pedal-axle

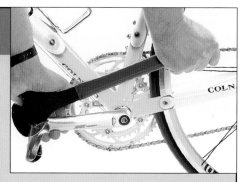

flats without risking damage to the cranks, and the length of the spanner provides sufficient leverage
when removing a stubborn pedal. Never use excessive force when installing a pedal, especially in an
alloy crank, as it is easy to damage threads.

To remove either pedal, turn the crank to face forward, level with the ground, and fit the spanner so
that it is angled above the crank, facing backwards. Now push down on the spanner, using your
body weight to help loosen the thread.

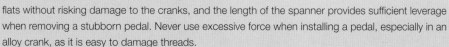

Clipless pedals

Time: 30 minutes
Grade of job: moderate
Equipment: bearing tool, vice, spanners, degreasing spray, replacement balls, grease, clean rag

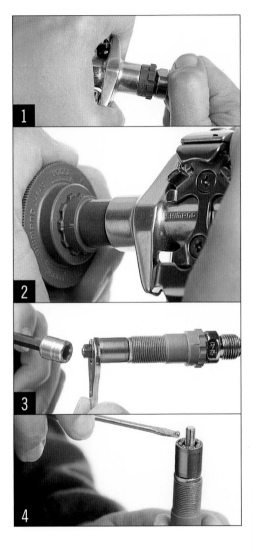

1 Pedal axles run in ball bearings, which can be serviced to extend their life. The axles in most clipless pedals may be removed, complete with bearings, using a special plastic tool supplied with the pedal.

2 Clamp the tool in a vice and turn the pedal, following the instruction arrow moulded into the plastic bearing housing. Traditional flat or quill pedals use cup-and-cone bearings, which are accessed by removing a cap on the outside of the pedal.

3 In either case, hold the pedal axle in a vice, using soft jaws to protect the thread. If the axle turns, hold it steady with the pedal spanner while slackening the lock-nut. Remove this and the cone-nut, and then pick the balls out with an old spoke. Note the assembly order and orientation of any small seals or washers. Allow the balls to drop on to kitchen towel or similar to avoid losing them, and clean all bearing parts using a clean rag and a degreasing spray. If any ball shows signs of corrosion or wear, replace all of them. Drop a sample ball bearing through the calibrated holes on a spoke rule to check their size.

4 Apply thick grease to the 'cup' bearing surfaces, and then sit the balls in place before reinstalling the axle and any washers. Install the cone nut, and then snug the lock-nut against it. There should be no play or binding in the bearing, so adjust as necessary. Tightening the lock-nut may affect play, so readjust if needed. Pack the bearings with more grease, then refit the cartridge or pedal cap.

5 Most clipless pedals have a small screw (two on a double-sided pedal) that allows adjustment of jaw spring tension. Experiment to find a comfortable resistance to exit. Make sure both sides are the same on a double-sided pedal by noting the position of the tension scale.

Cleats and shoes

There are many types of pedal and cleat, but all share one design feature; they can be adjusted fore and aft to place the ball of the foot over the pedal axle. Most can also be adjusted sideways to give clearance between the heel or ankle and crank. If fitting a new pedal and cleat system, follow the printed instructions on assembly order.

Installing cleats

Time: 15 minutes
Grade of job: moderate
Tools: Allen keys, screwdriver, grease

1 Ensure that the cleats and shoe are aligned the same way; most cleat systems are direction-specific.

2 Lightly grease the cleat mounting screws.

3 Place the cleat and assembly parts in order over the sole-mounting points, and install the screws. The Time TBT system employs two separate cleats per shoe; mount these individually.

4 Position the cleats on both shoes equidistant from the heel. Tighten the cleat screws, and go for a short ride.

5 Observe the position of the ball of the foot over the pedal axle. It may help to mark the position of the big toe joint on the outside of the shoe.

6 If necessary, slacken and adjust the cleat to place the ball of the foot directly over the pedal axle. At the same time, rotate the cleat as needed to angle the foot comfortably on the pedal. Many cleats allow 'float', making this last adjustment easier.

7 Tighten the cleat screws fully and adjust the pedal's cleat-retention screw as necessary.

Bars and stem

Conventional stems are of the quill type and are recognizable by the long tube that fits inside the steering bearing and fork. The threadless (or 'A-head') system is increasingly popular, and it may be recognized by its external clamp for the fork steerer-tube. Threadless forks and stems are made in 1in and 1⅛in diameters, and a shim must be used to adapt one to the other. Stems may have a twin-bolt, front-opening handlebar clamp for ease of assembly.

The important dimension when buying and fitting new bars or stem is that of the central bulge; this measurement must be identical on both components to ensure a secure clamping force.

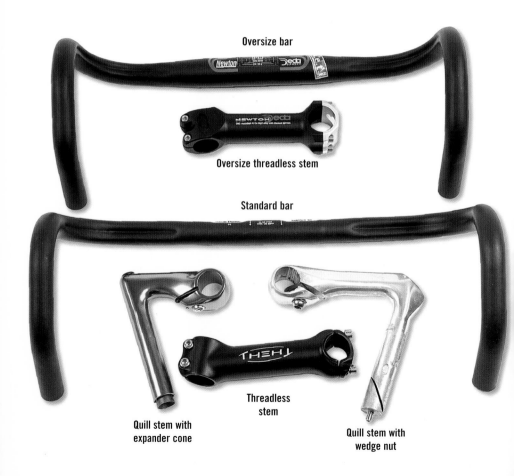

Oversize bar

Oversize threadless stem

Standard bar

Quill stem with
expander cone

Threadless
stem

Quill stem with
wedge nut

Installation of bars and stem

Time: 15 minutes
Grade of job: moderate
Tools: Allen keys, screwdriver, degreaser, grease

1 Clean and degrease the inside of the handlebar clamp and the surface of the handlebar bulge. Grease the clamp bolts and washers.

2 If fitting handlebars to a front-opening stem, ensure that, after tightening, there is an equal gap either side of the front cap.

3 To ease the fitting of a single-bolt stem to a curved bar, make sure that the chamfered indent in the clamp is on the inside of the curve. Some clamps allow the reversal of the bolt. If so, place a coin between the tip of the bolt and the face of the clamp, and tighten the bolt to spread the jaws of the clamp slightly. Do not over spread them.

4 Install the stem in the fork. Grease the quill and expander bolt thoroughly before installation. Pack spacers under and above a threadless stem before tightening it as described on page 99. By swapping the position of the washers, a comfortable handlebar height may be found before cutting the fork steerer-tube to length.

5 Decide on handlebar angle and tighten the bar clamp. Do not over-tighten, as this may damage light-alloy components.

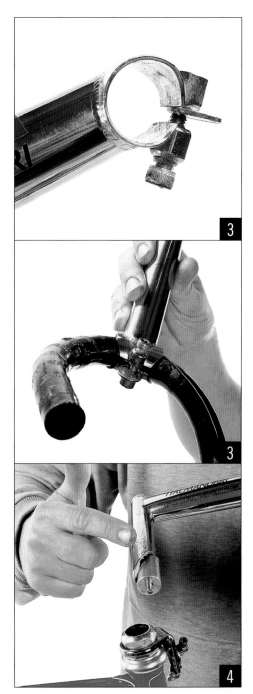

Handlebar tape

Neatly fitted handlebar tape is the finishing touch to any bike with dropped handlebars. There are many grades of bar tape, the best having a soft, grippy texture and an adhesive strip on the inside. For extra comfort, use a strip of old tape under the new tape in areas where the hands frequently rest.

Fitting bar tape

Time: 30 minutes
Grade of job: difficult
Tools: insulating tape, scissors

1 Tape control cables to the bars as described on page 43.

2 Pull back the lever rubbers and fit the small length of tape to the back of the brake lever, covering the clamp band.

3 Starting at the bottom of the bars, allow one tape width to overlap the end of the bar before starting to wind the tape.

4 Proceed in evenly spaced windings, maintaining an even tension on the tape.

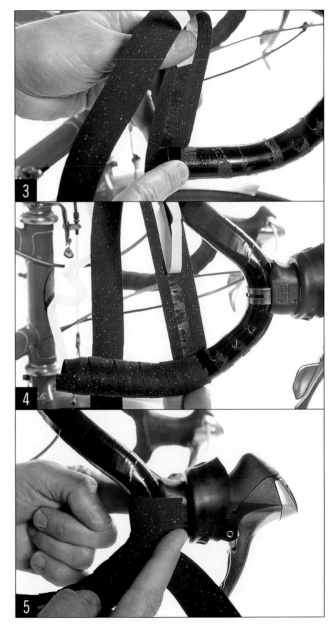

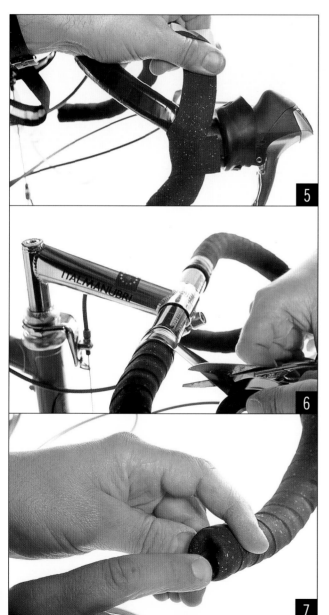

5 On reaching the brake lever, position the tape to fit exactly against the underside of the lever body, and wind it around the outside and over the top. Continue along the top of the bars, maintaining an even spacing on the outside of the bend.

6 On reaching the bar bulge, hold the tape at the angle it leaves the bar and cut perpendicular to the bar; this will leave a tapered strip. Wind this strip around the bar to leave a sharp edge, and finish off with a couple of turns of insulating tape.

7 Return the lever rubbers to their correct shape and fit the end plugs after stuffing the excess tape inside the end of the bar.

Saddle and seat post

Saddle shape undoubtedly affects ride comfort, but so too does the adjustment and alignment of your saddle and seat post. The saddle should be set parallel to the ground unless this position feels very uncomfortable, in which case a small tilt either way should be tried. When setting saddle height, raise or lower it until the knee is bent at roughly 25 to 30 degrees with the pedal at the bottom of its stroke. Make a gauge using a long piece of cardboard and a protractor to help check alignment. Set the middle of the saddle roughly in line with the centre-line of the frame seat tube. Adjust handlebar height and stem length to find a comfortable position.

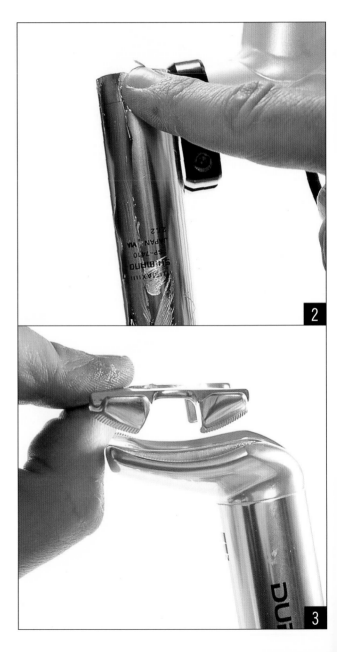

Installation and adjustment

Time: 10 minutes
Grade of job: easy
Tools: Allen keys, grease

1 Ensure that the inside of the frame's seat tube is clean and free of sharp burrs. Have it reamed by a shop if necessary.

2 Grease the seat post thoroughly, preferably with a non-metallic silicon grease, and insert the seat post to roughly the desired height. Tighten the seat-post clamp bolt.

3 Separate the parts of the saddle clamp, noting their order of installation.

4 Grease the clamp bolt threads.

5 Install the saddle and clamp, holding the various components until the bolt is in place.

6 Position the saddle in both planes and then tighten the bolt thoroughly. Check the angle and then test-ride the machine to ensure that it is comfortable.

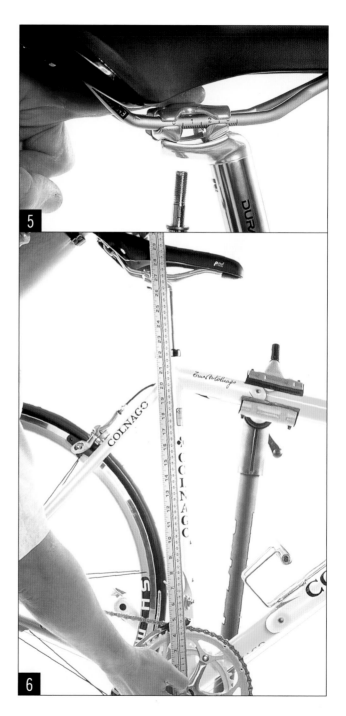

Frame checks

Repairs to the frame and fork are outside the scope of this book. Nonetheless, some checks are easily carried out. The main frame tubes, especially around the head tube and bottom-bracket shell, should be checked regularly for signs of cracks or deterioration. The same should be done around the rear-wheel dropouts. If the cycle is involved in a crash, roll the front wheel along a straight line to check wheel alignment. The rear wheel should follow precisely the same line. Measure and record the distance between the front wheel spindle and bottom-bracket axle. If the cycle is ridden into an obstacle, this dimension may be checked to tell if the front end is bent. A carbon-fibre fork involved in an impact should be replaced regardless of its apparent condition.

The headset

A bicycle depends on the steering bearing, or headset, for safe handling. There are two types: the traditional threaded headset; and the threadless, or 'A-head', type.

Maintenance of the headset

Time: 30 minutes
Grade of job: moderate
Tools: headset spanners, Allen keys, grease

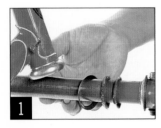

1 To strip a threaded headset, slacken the lock-nut and remove it along with any washers and the upper headset-nut complete with bearing race. The whole headset will now come apart for cleaning. Note the order of installation. Clean the races and balls with a degreasing spray and clean rag.

2 Grease the races and replace the balls or rollers. The headset shown uses caged rollers, which are simple to fit.

3 Refit the parts in order, installing the upper headset-nut and washers before fitting and tightening the lock-nut.

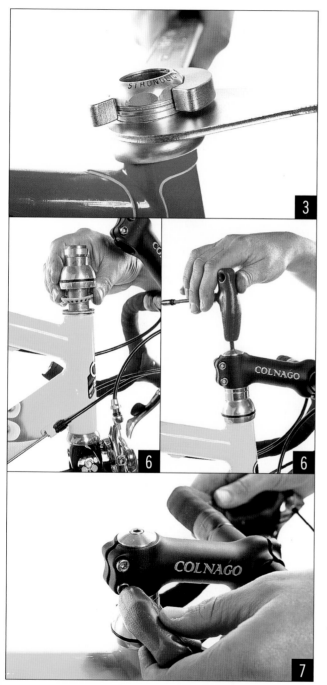

4 Refit the front wheel, bars and stem.

5 Apply the front brake and rock the machine back and forth to check for play. Adjust if necessary. Hold the front wheel off the ground and tap it sideways to check that the bearing turns easily. Slacken as needed. The headset is correctly adjusted when there is no slack and the fork turns freely. If the headset feels notchy, it is worn and must be replaced. Ask a mechanic to perform this complex task.

6 The threadless headset contains the same basic component parts, but is adjusted by tightening a top cap on to the stem, which in turn pushes on the top of the headset to compress the bearing and remove play. Any combination of stem and spacers must pack up to at least 3mm (⅛in) above the top of the steerer-tube to allow proper adjustment. Do not over-tighten the top cap, and check for free play frequently during adjustment. Ensure that the stem clamp is free before attempting to tighten the top cap.

7 Tighten the stem bolts securely after adjustment.

Fitting luggage

Anymore than the smallest load, such as a spare tube or lightweight waterproof, should be carried on the bicycle rather than the rider. The best way to carry any luggage is by attaching it to a rack; waterproofs may be simply strapped to the rack, while larger or heavier loads should be carried in panniers. To ensure safe handling, rear panniers should not be overloaded. A rough rule of thumb is to load each rear pannier with no more than 3kg (6½lbs), unless front panniers are also fitted. With front panniers attached, more weight may be added at the rear without fear of unbalancing the cycle. Always aim for even weight distribution between front and rear and on each side. Try to load heavy items first to keep weight low down.

It is preferable to attach a rack to special bosses brazed to the frame, rather than by clips, which are prone to break or scratch paintwork. Always stow loose straps carefully to avoid the risk of them tangling with a wheel.

Fitting panniers

Time: 15 minutes
Grade of job: moderate
Tools: Allen keys or screwdriver

1 Check the pannier fitments for sizing options. Many panniers are supplied with adaptors to ensure a snug fit on rack tubing of different diameters. If supplied, choose the correct fitting for the rack and install one to each of the top clips.

2 Adjust the two top clips to suit the rack. The ideal is to make the clips fit precisely between two cross-members, so that unwanted movement is impossible. The pannier does not have to be centred over the clips, but aim for a reasonable balance. It may prove necessary to position one or both of the clips outside the cross-members.

3 Remember that the rear pannier must be positioned far enough back to miss the heel of the shoe. Check either by measurement or by fitting a shoe to a pedal and aligning it directly.

4 Determine how the third attachment point works. There are numerous designs, so follow the literature supplied if unsure how it works. The pannier shown has a prong that can be moved around an oval track and turned to engage a strut of the rack. Try a selection of positions and choose the one that gives the most rigid, secure connection with the rack. The three attachments together should clip the pannier to the rack with minimal movement while also facilitating easy removal.

5 Repeat the process with the second pannier, getting it as close as possible to the same position as the first.

The rack's fitting screws should be checked for tightness frequently, especially when heavily laden, as a loose pannier rack can cause a dangerous wobble.

Mudguards

Many cyclists choose to ride without mudguards as they regard them as noisy and prone to breakage. However, well-fitted mudguards are both quiet and durable, and since they take much of the discomfort out of cycling in wet weather and on muddy roads, they are worth having on touring and utility bikes. Most are supplied as new with a mudflap behind the front wheel, which is usually the first part to break. Replace this with a piece of stiff plastic cut from a suitable food container, and pop-rivet it in place.

2

Fitting mudguards

Time: 30 minutes
Grade of job: moderate
Tools: spanner, Allen keys, hack saw, cable cutter, file, vice

1 Fit the mudguard clips to the cycle frame. On the rear guard, one clip will be attached to the chainstay bridge, the other to the rear-brake bridge. The latter must be positioned to suit the frame, and its lips crimped around the edge of the guard using pliers. The clip on the front guard is retained behind the fork crown with the brake's centre bolt.

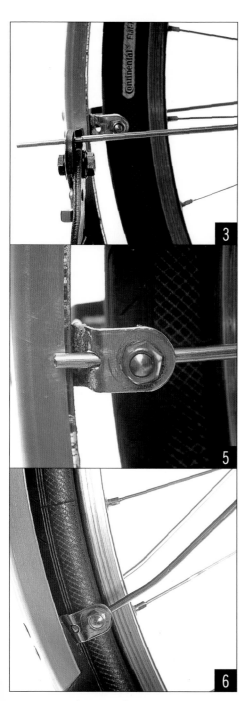

2 Fit one pair of stays to the first dropout or safety clip on the front fork, lightly tightening the small screw. Bend the two stays until they align with the two attachment points on the mudguard. If necessary, bend both stays in towards the guard so that they have an easy, unstressed run.

3 Align one stay with its attachment point and, while holding the guard at roughly the right distance from the tyre, mark a point about 6mm (¼in) further out using cable cutters. Do not attempt to cut the stay with the cutters. Repeat with the other stay.

4 Remove the stays from the frame, and cut through them at the marked points with a hacksaw. Remove any sharp edges with a file. Repeat for the opposite side.

5 Refit the stays on both sides, and at the attachment points install the small retaining screws. Adjust one side to clear the tyre as desired, and then do the same for the other side. The clearance for the tyre should be the same on both sides at all points. Ensure that the stay end does not protrude beyond the mudguard.

6 It may be necessary to bend the stays to achieve a straight run through the attachment points. The aim at all times is to finish with no residual stresses in the stays, so be prepared to bend them where needed. Check all nuts and bolts for tightness, and spin both wheels to check that no part of either mudguard rubs against a tyre.

Lighting

Cycle lighting comes in two basic types: it can be battery powered, in which case the durability of the lights is determined by the capacity of the batteries; or it can be powered by a dynamo, in which case the lighting system is entirely self-contained. Since the rider has to supply the power for a dynamo system, it will create some drag, which may amount to between two and three per cent of the cyclist's power.

In the most basic form of cycle lighting, the batteries are contained within the body of the lamp. Size constraints mean that battery capacity is limited and running time is, therefore, short, so it is a good idea to carry spare batteries. Such lights are lightweight, easy to fit and inexpensive. They can also be removed easily to prevent theft. Simple, battery-powered lighting is of most use on well-lit urban roads, and so the beam of the front lamp should be adjusted to attract the attention of motorists.

Battery-powered LED rear lights are both effective and inexpensive.

More powerful, but heavier, systems designed primarily for mountain biking have found favour with road cyclists. These systems, which can run for several hours, ally a bright headlamp with a separate rechargeable battery designed to hang from the frame or fit inside a bottle cage. However, rechargeable lights are expensive, and the weight of the batteries means that spares cannot easily be carried. The brightness of the headlamp means that it should not be aimed at motorists' eye level.

A lightweight halogen front lamp will provide adequate illumination for most road cyclists.

Once fitted, dynamo systems need no maintenance, and since they are an integral part of the cycle they are rarely stolen. Many are designed to use the frame as the earth for electrical current. However, it is always better to use double-axis cable for all the wiring in a dynamo system.

Aligning a bottle dynamo

Time: 5 minutes
Grade of job: easy
Tools: metre rule, spanners

1 Install the dynamo, using either the brace supplied or any frame bosses provided for the purpose. Flip the dynamo to the on position so that it rubs against the side of the tyre. Move it up or down until the wheel runs against the centre of the tyre sidewall.

2 Align a metre rule or other straight edge through the centre-line of the dynamo, and move the dynamo on its bracket until the edge of the rule runs directly through the centre of the front-wheel spindle.

3 Check that the dynamo wheel still runs centrally on the sidewall before tightening all fittings.

Troubleshooting

 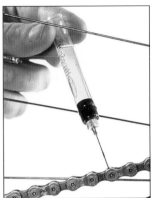

Symptom	Cause
Excessive pressure from saddle	Saddle not level/Saddle wrong shape
Knees ache	Saddle wrong height/Pedals incorrectly aligned/Pedal axle or crank bent
Wrists/shoulders ache	Handlebars wrong height/too stretched
Steering vague	Headset too tight/Front tyre soft
Chain jumps	Stiff link
Gears won't shift	Maladjusted mech
Rhythmic creaking noise when pedalling	Loose chainring bolt/Dry pedal cleat/Loose crank bolt
Creaking noise when pulling on handlebars	Dryness or corrosion around stem
Wobble at speed	Slack spokes/Poor headset adjustment/Poor hub adjustment/Frame weakness
'Soggy' feel to transmission	Worn chain and sprockets
Snatching when brake is applied	Rim dented or about to split

Remedy

Ensure saddle is level/Change saddle

Reset saddle height/Realign pedals/Ask shop to check pedals or crank

Alter bar position

Adjust headset, inflate tyre

Find and ease stiff link, lubricate chain

Check adjustment

Check tightness of all bolts/Apply grease to cleat mating faces/Strip and reassemble crankset

Remove stem, clean and grease quill

Check spoke tension and wheel trueness/Adjust bearings/Check frame and fork for cracks

Replace chain and sprockets as necessary

Check condition of rim and renew as necessary

Glossary

Anatomic bars
Dropped 'racing' handlebars with a lower section specially shaped to fit the hand.

Bead of tyre
Steel wire or Kevlar cord moulded into the edge of the tyre to hold it on to the rim.

Bearings
Rolling elements within rotating parts designed to reduce friction – balls are usually used in bicycle bearings.

Bowden cables
Control cables comprising a thin flexible inner wire and incompressible outer casing.

Caliper (brake)
Part of brake assembly that closes on a pivot to press friction pads against the wheel rim.

Cartridge (bearing)
Bearing assembly in which balls or rollers and their races are contained in one non-separable unit.

Chain stays
Frame tubes running either side of the rear wheel between the wheel spindle and bottom bracket axle.

Cleat
Shaped piece attached to the sole of a cycling shoe to engage with the jaws of clipless pedals. May be made from metal or plastic.

Clipless pedals

A range of automatic-release pedal designs in which the shoe is secured to the pedal by a cleat trapped in jaws. This does away with the traditional toeclip and strap, hence 'clipless'.

Crank

One of the arms to which the pedals are attached. The cranks rotate around the bottom bracket axle.

Cutting threads

Screw threads are usually formed by cutting into the parent material. A male (external) thread is cut using a die, a female thread using a tap. Spoke threads are formed by rolling.

Dog

Short projection parallel to the central axis on a rotating component. Engages with matching projection(s) on another part on the same axis.

Downtube

The main cycle frame tube running diagonally from the steerer tube to the bottom bracket axle.

Drift

Any length of material held against a component to be driven by hammering the other end of the drift. May be used to protect the component or to apply the force of the hammer in a confined space.

Dropouts

the slotted plates at the ends of the stays and fork blades. The wheels 'drop out' when their securing nuts or quick release mechanisms are undone.

ErgoPower shifter

Dual control lever unit from Campagnolo of Italy which combines gear shifting and braking functions in one lever.

Pedal float

Free play in a clipless pedal system that allows the heel to move in or out allowing the foot to find a comfortable pedalling alignment.

Freehub

Rear hub design in which the freewheel mechanism is located within the hub itself, rather than in a separate body.

Groupset

Term for collection of cycle components from one manufacturer, usually including chainset, gears, brakes and hubs, and with one common model name.

Hanger

Projection from rear gearside dropout which holds the rear mech.

Hex nut

Six-sided nut.

Hub flange

One of the discs at each end of a hub at which the spokes are attached.

Indexed gearing

System of derailleur gear control where each gear is selected by precise positioning of the control lever or mechanism. As opposed to friction shifting, where gears are selected by rider skill.

Mech

Mechanism designed to derail the drive chain from one sprocket or chainwheel to another.

Nipple

Bulb on the end of a thin wire to allow it to be pulled or held in tension. May be metal cast on to an inner control wire, or threaded to permit tensioning of a spoke.

Noodle pipe

Curved tube used on V-brakes as part of the outer casing.

Pawls

Spring-loaded moving teeth within a freewheel mechanism to permit free running in one direction only.

Shimano HG tool

Chain breaking tool design specifically for use with Shimano HyperGlide chains.

Soft jaws

Placed over the jaws of a vice, and made of soft metal or fibre to protect the finish of parts held in the vice.

Spider

Arrangement of arms – usually five – radiating from the right-hand crank, and supporting the chainrings.

Splined tool

Tool formed with radiating ridges designed to mate with matching grooves on component to be turned using force on the tool.

Steerer tube

Tube concealed within the head tube, connecting the fork crown and handlebar stem.

Stem

Length of tube connecting the handlebars and steerer tube.

STI shifter

Dual control lever unit from Shimano of Japan which combines gear shifting and braking functions in one lever.

Straight-push cramp

Special type of pliers where the two jaws approach straight on, instead of through an arc.

Throw adjuster screw

One of a pair of small screws used on rear mech to limit its range of movement, and prevent the chain being thrown off the end sprockets or chainrings.

Trim (as in gears)

Act of adjusting poorly-aligned front mech to prevent the chain rubbing on the cage.

Index

Acknowledgements

All photography Octopus Publishing Group Limited/Gerard Brown except for the following:
Octopus Publishing Group Limited/Tim Woodcock 46, 47 top, 47 bottom, 60, 61 top, 61 bottom, 84 left, 84 right, 88 top right, 88 bottom right, 88 centre right top, 88 centre right bottom

Executive editor Trevor Davies
Editor Rachel Lawrence
Design manager Tokiko Morishima
Designer Martin Topping
Production controller Ian Paton
Special photography Gerard Brown
Index compiled by Indexing Specialists

Special thanks to Caroline Griffiths of **Madison Cycles** for providing the equipment featured in this publication.